D1756779

General Editor: Robin Gilmour

PETER QUARTERMAINE

Senior Lecturer,
School of English and American Studies,
University of Exeter

Edward Arnold

A division of Hodder & Stoughton
LONDON NEW YORK MELBOURNE AUCKLAND

© Peter Quartermaine

First published in Great Britain 1991

Distributed in the USA by Routledge, Chapman and Hall, Inc.
29 West 35th Street, New York, NY 10001

British Library Cataloguing in Publication Data

Quartermaine, Peter
  Thomas Keneally. – (Modern fiction)
  I. Title II. Series
  823

ISBN 0-340-51826-X

Typeset in 10/12pt Linotron Sabon by
Hewer Text Composition Services, Edinburgh
Printed and bound in Great Britain for Edward Arnold,
a division of Hodder and Stoughton Limited,
Mill Road, Dunton Green, Sevenoaks, Kent TN13 2YA by
Biddles Ltd, Guildford & King's Lynn

Contents

*To my Mother
and
The Memory of my Father*

General Editor's Preface

Fiction constitutes the largest single category of books published each year, and the discussion of fiction is at the heart of the present revolution in literary theory, yet the reader looking for substantial guidance to some of the most interesting prose writers of the twentieth century – especially those who have written in the past 30 or 40 years – is often poorly served. Specialist studies abound, but up-to-date maps of the field are harder to come by. *Modern Fiction* has been designed to supply that lack. It is a new series of authoritative introductory studies of the chief writers and movements in the history of twentieth-century fiction in English. Each volume has been written by an expert in the field and offers a fresh and accessible reading of the writer's work in the light of the best recent scholarship and criticism. Biographical information is provided, consideration of the writer's relationship to the world of their times, and detailed readings of selected texts. The series includes short-story writers as well as novelists, contemporaries as well as the classic moderns and their successors, Commonwealth writers as well as British and American; and there are volumes on themes and groups as well as on individual figures. At a time when twentieth-century fiction is increasingly studied and talked about, *Modern Fiction* provides short, helpful, stimulating introductions designed to encourage fresh thought and further enquiry.

Robin Gilmour

Preface

Special thanks to my old friend Alastair Niven for introducing me to this Series; and my gratitude to Robin Gilmour for being a General Editor as accessible and helpful in human terms as he was distant geographically.

Some research for this book was carried out in Australia during 1988, thanks to a research fellowship from the Sir Robert Menzies Centre for Australian Studies, London, and a grant from the University of Exeter Research Committee; I am properly grateful to both institutions for their invaluable support.

For genial Australian hospitality I am indebted to John and Nan Vasey (not forgetting Ruth), to Brian Seidel and to Alan and Carol Lawson. Staff at The Fryer Library, University of Queensland, and at the National Library of Australia, Canberra, were unfailingly helpful in answering my queries – and suggesting others. My Australian undergraduate student Dixie Stiles kindly read and commented on the Introduction, and Thomas Keneally was helpful in providing – and correcting – dates and details in the Chronological Table.

My thanks once again to David and Mary Alice Lowenthal for their haven on a hill during my researches in London.

Chapter 3 is developed from a seminar paper delivered at the Sir Robert Menzies Centre as 'Options in the Shadow of History: *The Chant of Jimmie Blacksmith*' which was published in *Aspects of Commonwealth Literature, Volume 1* (Institute of Commonwealth Studies, 1990), edited by Dr Liz Gunner.

Opinions expressed in this book are mine alone, except where otherwise acknowledged; I accept full credit for all errors.

A Note on Editions

Reference throughout is to paperback editions of novels, published by Penguin (*The Chant of Jimmie Blacksmith* and *Three Cheers for the Paraclete*), Coronet (*Confederates*) and Sceptre (*Schindler's Ark* and *The Playmaker*).

Art is the principal means by which a human tries to compensate for, or complement, the relentlessness of death and temporality.

Alex Colville

1

Introduction

The reasons for initiating the system of transportation of felons to Australia have been written about a good deal – badly in the textbooks whose pages we turned in the humid classrooms of our Australian childhood summers. . . . I studied Goldsmith's 'The Deserted Village' [1770], though it was not pointed out to me that some of the people from 'The Deserted Village' were probably in [Governor Arthur] Phillip's convict transports.
(Thomas Keneally, *Australia, Beyond the Dreamtime*)

In an important sense Thomas Keneally needs no introduction. Communicative and lively by nature as befits his Irish ancestry (of which he is very proud), his written work has an immediacy, pace and variety which draws the reader into events depicted, whether battles in fifteenth-century France or nineteenth-century America, war in Nazi Germany or in present-day Eritrea (the African country in which his 1989 *Towards Asmara* is set). A character in *The Chant of Jimmie Blacksmith* (1972) envies the public hangman in that book his 'ringside seat to history', and Keneally's fiction often aims to satisfy that yen for a more direct knowledge of 'history' which we can all admit to. The ways in which Keneally undertakes that challenge as a writer, and the extent to which he succeeds, are explored in this book. But what of the man himself? And, more important, how far does knowing more about the man help us in reading his books?

Thomas Keneally was born in Sydney, Australia, in 1935 into an Irish Catholic family, but spent his first seven years on the coast to the north, in the towns of Kempsey, Wauchope and Taree. In 1942 the family moved to Strathfield, a western suburb of Sydney. Educated by the Christian Brothers at St Patrick's College, Strathfield, he decided

– despite protests from his parents – to study for the priesthood at St Patrick's College, Manly: 'my leaving coincided with the death of Pius XII, but it didn't have a casual link with it'. (Keneally recalls Pius XII as dying in 'about 1959'. In fact it was in 1958; he himself abandoned study for the priesthood in 1960.) For some time Keneally worked as a builder's labourer in the Riverina area of South Western New South Wales, then returned to Sydney and 'worked with the Department of Territories for about four or five months, buying machettes for New Guinea and so on'.

It was after this period that Keneally became a schoolteacher, a job which continued until he became a professional writer. His first book, *The Place at Whitton*, was published in 1964, and after this he took a job collecting insurance money 'weekly or fortnightly in small sums' from poor or working class people in industrial suburbs of Sydney – Newtown, Enmore and Petersham (the middle class, Keneally recalls, paid their premiums yearly or half-yearly). This work occupied Keneally for about two days a week, and the rest of the time he had free for writing; he remembers this period as being 'very instructive'. Winning the national Miles Franklin Award for literature in 1967 with *Bring Larks and Heroes* enabled him to become a full-time writer; *Three Cheers for the Paraclete*, which traces a young priest's conflicts with his superiors, won the prize the following year. In 1965 Keneally married Judith Martin: they have two daughters, Margaret (b.1966) and Jane (b.1967).

Today Keneally is Australia's best-known writer. He travels widely, writes frequently in the Australian press on a wide range of topics, appears on television and clearly thrives on seminars, panel discussions and university workshops, however much he may doubt their relevance to his innermost concerns: 'although I am flattered to do interviews for literary magazines . . . I feel like a bit of an impostor because I am a commercial writer'. Keneally is rightly proud that his books sell well – that is, that they are actually *read* by a large number of people – but in some respects, despite the familiar smiling face, Keneally remains a very private person in his concerns, and wary of the effects of publicity. This book will suggest that the reasons for a guarded – and perfectly understandable – privacy beyond the carefully-circumscribed smiling 'personality' may, in Keneally's case at least, be more than usually relevant to the concerns and methods of his fictions. One consideration here is that of Keneally's position as an Australian, a country which is more than usually subject to being viewed in stereotypical ways, at least in Britain and the United States. As the English novelist Peter Ackroyd rightly commented in

1977: 'Keneally is an Australian writer, and this plays a large though unacknowledged role in his writings'.

There is a long history of views (literally) of Australia being produced by itinerant English artists for consumption back 'home' in London; the professional artists appointed to accompany Captain James Cook on his three voyages of exploration to the Pacific between 1768 and 1779 furnished the first such views. Today a strange combination of *Neighbours* (whose viewing figures in Britain exceed the population of Australia) and films such as *Crocodile Dundee* perform a similar function in terms of the popular imagination. Subsequently the view that Australians took of the world, and of their own position in it, was largely shaped by determination to construct 'a new Britannia' in the South Hemisphere which would outdo the old in vigour, in wealth *and* in Britishness. Such was one important strand in the culture which the young Keneally would have inherited – along with post-Federation Australian nationalism and Irish culture (at one remove). It is a powerful, and at times deeply contradictory, mix.

A consequence of being a writer in a country such as Australia which has a relatively small population (some 17 million) and a comparatively recent history of settlement is that every book or utterance is attributed a greater significance than would be the case in a larger and more disparate nation. This has good effects and bad. It is good in that the writer or artist can easily assume a prominence in public life which would be hard to parallel in Britain; Australians can be fiercely proud of their writers and artists, and exhibitions and galleries are visited by large numbers of people (far more than attend public sporting fixtures). Such popularity can have a hard price, though, from the writers' point of view, in that they may feel a pressure to conform to some consensus view of what is suitably 'Australian'.

To be that imperilled creature 'an Australian writer', then, is unavoidably to mix public (even national) roles and private passions, for as Keneally himself wryly expresses the problem: 'every book that an Australian writes is a potential contribution to the body of AUST. LIT. [Australian Literature] and if you disappoint a reviewer you are not just disappointing the reviewer you are committing an act of national dereliction.' His own generation was still brought up to regard the two terms 'Australian' and 'writer' as mutually exclusive. Asked why he became a novelist, Keneally replied that as a child it was something he 'felt most alienated from. As colonials we were raised on British literature and it had very little connection with what we saw around us ... it seemed such an extraordinary thing to be a novelist'. A predictable result of such a 'colonial education' was that the hemisphere in which he lived seemed 'outside literature', and he responded to 'the challenge of ... trying to bring this continent on the literary map'.

Drawing analogies with the early novels (in the late 1940s and early 1950s) of fellow Australian novelist Patrick White (1921–1990), Keneally has said that writing about his own country was for him 'a sort of coming to terms with your surroundings', the result of a sense of alienation which was accentuated by education: 'All the books we read were full of trees we had never seen, most of our schooling was about places that we knew nothing of and had never seen. We were actually educated to be exiles.' Such an education is subtly cruel, and its effects likely to be lasting; Keneally confessed in 1967 – the year that *Bring Larks and Heroes* was published – that he was 'obsessed with the notion of Australia as a country alien to the people who live in it'. Significantly, he added, 'Why, I don't know. I'm certainly not alien to it. I've never lived anywhere else.'[1] The Conclusion to this study will suggest some ways in which Keneally's 'Australianness' has led to his being simultaneously praised and misread by many overseas critics.

Keneally's memories of 'education for alienation' confirm the experience of several other Commonwealth writers of his generation, that at school 'literature' was, by definition, something that came from – and dealt with – Britain. The Trinidadian novelist Sir V.S. Naipaul (born 1932) once recalled that at school even the look and smell of certain London-published textbooks were inextricably associated in his mind with 'literature' (in which snow in Dickens was accepted not as fact but as 'a literary convention'), while for the white South African writer Nadine Gordimer (born 1923) growing up in a small South African town, the word 'intellectual' actually *meant* 'someone from abroad'. She was quite sure that there were no intellectuals in South Africa, not because local talent was of insufficient quality but because the term quite simply couldn't apply.

Such shared experiences, and the writings which reflect them, are a useful framework within which to approach Keneally's changing sense of his craft and role; the two are inextricably related. He describes

---

1. Laurie Clancy, 'Thomas Keneally's Three Novels', *Meanjin* 112, XXVII, 1968, pp.33–41, reference on p.37. Reprinted in *Australian Postwar Novelists: Selected Critical Essays*, ed. Nancy Keesing (Jacaranda Press, Brisbane), 1975, pp.57–67. Reference on p.63.

himself as still 'fairly young and callow' when *The Chant of Jimmie Blacksmith* appeared in 1972, but already he saw the 'fairly drab' culture around him as a challenge to his creative abilities: 'it seemed to me as if Australian society had crushed out something beautiful or at least something well ordered, mainly the aboriginal society, . . . to replace it with a great suburban nullity'.[2]

Acutely aware of the cultural imperialism which shaped his early education – 'we were raised to be loyal cannon fodder for the British Empire' – Keneally was to find that this world changed more quickly than he could have predicted. The year 1942 saw not only his family move to Sydney, but also the fall of the British outpost of Singapore to the Japanese, an unthinkable event which, as Keneally puts it, 'cancelled' the British Empire in his part of the world. He recalls a childhood memory of that period, of a ferry trip from the small resort of Manly (near the entrance of Sydney Harbour) to the city of Sydney itself:

> The first time I made this wonderful journey from Manly to Sydney – at least the first time that I remember – was as a child down from the bush in 1942. The Japanese were at that stage revealing our Asian location to us by bombing some of our more tropical ports like Darwin and Broome, and the *Queen Mary* – loaded with troops newly returned from their rather remote imperial duty in the Middle East – was poking its way through the Harbour's august heads.
> (*Beyond the Dreamtime*, 17)

Japanese victories against the British in the Pacific were eventually to open Australia to the increasing cultural, economic and military influence of the United States, one bitter fruit of which was later to be Australia's involvement in the Vietnam War from 1965 until the election of Gough Whitlam as Labour Prime Minister in December 1972. The searing physical and moral brutalities of the Vietnam period, and its impact upon Australia's tender sense of national identity and purpose, Keneally explored indirectly in *Bring Larks and Heroes*.

One effect of these overarching cultural shifts may well have been to make Keneally wary of over-exposure in terms of local and national themes, and so to set his books at an historical and geographical distance from his home base. This said, there is no sense that

---

2. Interview with Thomas Keneally by Rudi Krausmann. *Aspect* 4/1–2, 1979, pp.48–58. Reference on p.52. The next four quotations by Keneally are also from this article; page references are given in the text.

Keneally has avoided the controversial. The intense and shared human experiences of sex and sudden death (the latter, at least, intimately described) recur in much of Keneally's writings, and although many of the later books locate such experiences in contexts historically and geographically remote from Australia, there were also locally-set precursors. Keneally explored some of the issues relating to the early period of Australian-United States relations immediately following the fall of Singapore in his 1980 novel *The Cut Rate Kingdom*, which broke new publishing ground (with no commercial success) by being produced in the format of a colour magazine, with text and 'period' photographs fully integrated. He has said of this time that it was marked politically by 'Something that is very strongly in the Australian soul somewhere, if there is an Australian soul', namely the great 'Utopian dream of making a sort of new society in the South Seas'.[3] A similar ambition underlay some of the imaginative initiatives launched by Whitlam after his election in 1972, but certainly his period of office (until November 1975) was remarkable for the new feeling of Australian self-awareness and identity which it stimulated on many fronts, and not least in the arts through the establishment in 1973 of the Australia Council to promote and fund cultural activities on a national basis. This work continues today, and is one in which Keneally himself has been actively involved, sitting on several committees.

The sense of institutionalised alienation that Keneally remembers so keenly from those 'humid classrooms' of childhood was increasingly to be replaced by national interest and pride in the richness and diversity of Australian culture. In literature the award of the Nobel Prize for Literature to Patrick White in 1973 was indirectly of immense importance in alerting readers (and publishers) to a wealth of new talent in Australia; it was of relevance directly, too, for White used the money to set up a fund for awards to distinguished young Australian writers. Keneally's own works, certainly after the publication of *Jimmie Blacksmith*, played a major part in raising the profile of Australian literature internationally. Such profound reassessment of cultural identity attracted enhanced worldwide attention in the 1970s through the 'new wave' of Australian cinema; *The Chant of Jimmie Blacksmith* was itself filmed in 1978 by the Australian director Fred Schepisi (an old friend), Keneally himself playing with relish the rogue Irish cook on the outback station.

If there is an interesting case for considering Keneally's fiction at

3. Thomas Keneally, 'Doing Research For Historical Novels', *The Australian Author*, 7/1, 1975, pp.27–9. Reference on p.27.

least partly in the context of his background, nationality and location, these are not the terms in which debate about the books has been conducted (or, indeed, the terms in which the books themselves have mostly posed questions). Critical concern has been more with wide-ranging questions of authorial stance and the process of writing than with specific biographical or regional considerations. Such a line of debate, while useful and proper, and one which may well match Keneally's own preferences, is not necessarily the most revealing approach. Asked in 1979 for whom he wrote, Keneally admitted this to be 'a great problem', and pointed out that he had 'written popular books with moderate success', as well as 'more experimental' texts (here he instanced his 1979 novel *Passenger*). His more general response, though, was to suggest that 'writers have this sense of alienation' largely because of 'a poisonous idea', originating with the Romantics, that 'art is special, separate and so on'.[4]

Keneally's preferred role is that of an individual who practises a craft, believing as he does that until modern times 'art was more functional, it was something that happened daily . . . when illiterate stonemasons took a chisel to stone'. In such periods, he maintains, art was 'a daily not a compartmentalised thing. It wasn't something you did for a council and it wasn't something that people did with the devotional air with which they do it now.'[5] This belief that art should be fun, rather than experienced with 'a sense of merit, not with a sense of enjoyment', informs both Keneally's choice of subject matter and his approach to it. In similar vein he stresses his delight in watching sport on television: 'That's a very un-Australian thing. Australian society is roughly divided between those who have ideas and those who play sport but I don't find that there is any barrier between the two'. With a house overlooking Potts Point in Sydney and another on the coast, Keneally – an asthmatic as a child – is now able to enjoy his love of swimming and surfing to the full. The sea he finds wonderfully 'rejuvenative and therapeutic, the best possible place to go. . . . It gives gaiety but mainly gives something more important and that's serenity.' Typically, he cannot resist adding, 'But I like talking and drinking too'. Such stated interests and enjoyments locate him firmly in the mainstream of Australian popular culture; a man of the people.

4. Bob Ellis, 'Thomas Keneally, The Wizard of Oz Lit', *Times on Sunday* [Australia], 11 October 1987, pp.25 and 26. I am grateful to Katherine Gallagher for this reference.
5. Krausmann, p.56.

Such life and leisure activities may be Keneally's way of life, but it is not a way of life that he writes about; we learn very little about contemporary Australia from his prodigious fiction output, though he has contributed to the book of a BBC television series on the country, *Australia: Beyond the Dreamtime*, 1987. There is, of course, no obligation for a writer or artist to reflect the immediate context of composition, and the imaginative dimensions of art (not to mention the histories of art and literature) would be sorely constrained if there were. Keneally's recorded attitudes to his chosen profession of writer are easy-going and somewhat unconventional. Asked for his reaction to literary debate in Europe on whether the novel was dead he replied: 'We in Australia have enough trouble coming to terms with its existence, let alone its death, but the novel seems very much alive to me'. Alive it might be, but Keneally was quick to stress changes in the novel's form and function; he instances the 'pluralism' and 'moral ambiguity' of modern society as conditions which militated against 'those sure rock solid forms in which nineteenth- and eighteenth-century novelists wrote', and admitted that 'The conventional novel is dead in the sense that it doesn't serve a purpose except as a preparatory movie script or as a preparatory television script'.[6]

This is a large and problematic contention, especially in the context of a book such as *Schindler's Ark* (1982) which straddles the genres of fiction and documentary but which has yet to be filmed (though Hollywood director Steven Speilberg has bought the film rights to the book). Not only is Keneally's view of the eighteenth- and nineteenth-century novel somewhat simplistic, but his own most exciting (and controversial) blendings of fact and fiction themselves have well-established precedents in earlier literature. His writing has sometimes attracted hostile criticism for its assumed courting of Hollywood's attentions, but Keneally seems interested not so much in film in its own right as in establishing serious fiction as widely enjoyable. This is a reasonable enough aim; after all, no one questions the 'seriousness' of Shakespeare's comedies, which were equally popular in their day.

A conspicuous quality of Keneally's writing is its preoccupation with the past and, looking from Sydney, with the foreign, as setting. Of his novels to date, only the early, and partly autobiographical, works – *The Place at Whitton* (1964), *The Fear* (1965) and *Three Cheers for the Paraclete* (1968) – have depicted a society of which he could claim

6. Krausmann, p.49.

intimate knowledge. Other books – *A Victim of the Aurora* (1977) and *Passenger* (1979) especially – can be seen as touching directly upon contemporary life, but otherwise only *A Family Madness* (1985) confronts directly the everyday life of the Sydney suburbs, a culture in which Keneally himself grew up after 1942 – and in this novel the Sydney context is juxtaposed with a typically vivid recreation of an emigrant family's wartime memories of Belorussia. *Towards Asmara*, though, showed the dangers of easy generalisations where Keneally's work is concerned, with its topical (if unconvincing) exploration of contemporary Eritrean politics.

Shortly after the publication of *Blood Red, Sister Rose* in 1974, Keneally contributed an interview to *The Australian Author* for a series on the methods writers used in carrying out research, in his case research for historical novels. He began by distinguishing between research for historical fiction and for scholarly purposes:

> If you're writing fiction you have one of two attitudes to history. You wish either to point out the quaintness or exotic quality of a time past – to create a sort of travelogue to another time having little relevance to ours; or else you want to find evidence in earlier events for the kind of society we have now, wishing to tell a parable about the present by using the past. I attempt the latter.[7]

A crucial difference, as Keneally sees it, between the approaches of the scholarly historian and of the novelist is that whereas the historian must 'prove his reliability to other scholars and to his readers' the 'only warrant a novelist needs for his ideas about the past is that they reek of human, poetic, dramatic, symbolic veracity and resound in his imagination'. Keneally gleefully admits that such a distinction must 'sound scandalous to historians', but contends that while 'in some ways novelists are the worst historians', some of them 'might turn out to be the best historians of all'. At another level, though, the use of the term 'parable' by Keneally signals an aspect of his writings which cannot be ignored: their enduring engagement with human and moral dilemmas which can properly only be termed religious. Keneally withdrew from his planned devotion to the religious life, but – hardly surprisingly – the training of those years have left their mark upon the preoccupations that characterise his creative work.

It has been suggested by an Australian writer and critic who knows him well, and who sees him as 'A long way from his home town parish

---

7. 'Doing Research for Historical Novels', p.27.

and glad of the distance', that Keneally's avoidance of contemporary settings is due at least in part 'to his distaste for making enemies: those close mates he has (often fellow seminarians like Ed Campion, Brian Johns, Fred Schepisi) he has kept, and cherished, lifelong'.[8] Keneally's own emphasis is – as we have seen – different, more concerned with form and meaning than with friends or foes, though his argument does suggest a caution, even a conservatism, in its reading of the past as 'parables' for the present: 'writers will always be attracted by the past. It is less confusing than the present. Historians have already reduced it to some understandable unity for us. Their gift is beyond estimation.' In seeing the past as 'easier to handle than the perilous moment in which we live', Keneally is also quick to stress that it 'nonetheless has massive relevance for us . . . it is the present merely rendered fabulous'.

The extent to which 'the past' that Keneally treats in his work is mostly a European (certainly a Northern Hemisphere) past may be seen as a further example of his wariness in handling material closer to hand – or simply a recognition that historically and culturally the past of Europe is also the past of Australia; Keneally's own Irish ancestry makes him specially aware of this, and at the same time distances him from any easy identification with 'England'. In *Towards Asmara* there are suggestions that Australia and Africa have much in common, and one critic has observed that '*Schindler's Ark* is a peculiarly Australian book, owing more to the mythology of the bush than to that of central Europe'.[9] For Keneally's part, it would seem that the hindsight afforded uniquely by an historical perspective both aids and stimulates his own search for unity, though critics have varied widely in their assessment of his success.

Keneally argues that the 'sequence of historic events does not count as much as the novelist's necessity to create his own world out of the material he finds', adding 'It must be a valid world, mind you, and it must take account of the way events occurred and their order'. An important aspect of the way in which Keneally creates this 'valid world' has to do with what he terms 'quotidian things . . . what loungesuit they were likely to hanker for, what they would have in the wardrobe (in the way of garments I mean, not drink), whether they put rinse in their hair, what they used for piles, what they considered a healthy baby, what were their funerary rites'. On

8. Ellis, p.26.
9. Michael Hollington, 'The Ned Kelly of Cracow: Keneally's *Schindler's Ark*', *Meanjin* 42, I, March 1983, pp.42–6. Reference on p.42.

suchlike items 'the newspapers of the day are beyond value. . . . For newspapers – inaccurate and all – are full of the common savour of life.' In Keneally's fiction what he terms such a 'reek' or 'savour' is conveyed through a detailed imaginative recreation of person and place, a process which is part of our normal historical sense. David Lowenthal writes as follows in *The Past is a Foreign Country* of this sensibility:

> Historical consciousness is enlarged also by surmises about unrecorded events and those for which records are lost or destroyed; by speculations about a past which might some day happen, or one which could never have happened, like an encounter between Tamerlane and Joan of Arc; and by counter-factual ruminations generally.[10]

We must distinguish, though, between the clarity with which Keneally recreates such situations and that 'understandable unity' to which historians 'reduce' the past. In his fiction the former owes its power to the novelist's inventive talents for characterisation and dialogue, whereas the latter is largely a deductive process from a posited position. David Lowenthal stresses that historical knowledge does indeed tell us 'things about the past not known to those who lived at the time' (p.214), but only because what was their present is a dimension of our past: too late we know not to book a cabin on the *Titanic*, but take statistically greater risks each day in crossing the road. An alertness to this effect of the passing of time – what we might term the 'hindsight of mortality' – is reflected in Keneally's describing the past as 'a parable for the present'; It conveys – or can be made to convey, whether by historian or novelist – certain hints, directions and lessons for the present age. The crucial question, raised directly by the Biblical term 'parable', is that of the pattern of beliefs according to which such a parable is to be read in order for it to reveal its deeper meaning. It is this attributed *meaning* which has the power to affect our present.

If the past attracts the novelist by being 'less confusing' than the present, by being 'reduced', it also offers the complementary fascination of being forever completely unknowable since, as Lowenthal puts it, 'the sheer pastness of the past precludes its total reconstruction' (p.216). To hold the reader's attention, and to structure events which

10. David Lowenthal, *The Past is a Foreign Country*. Cambridge University Press 1985, Cambridge, p.211, footnote 162. This book is a very readable and rewarding exploration of changing attitudes to the past, and how these affect our understanding of both present and future.

– at the time – seemed as random as do our own daily lives, the historian employs the narrative devices of the traditional novel: plot; character; setting; action. A moral – or 'conclusion' – is also often drawn. In these respects, then, Keneally is not as far removed from the scholarly historian's methods as he (or the historian) might hope. Moreover, both inevitably bring to their interest in, and understanding of, the past a spectrum of modern assumptions, both individual and general. As Lowenthal expresses it: 'Just as we are products of the past, so is the past an artifact of ours' (p.216). This truth is never more clearly illustrated than at election times, when politicians seek votes on the basis of widely differing pasts, for which they claim credit or attribute blame. Our eventual vote is determined as much by belief in a past as hopes for a future.

From this examination of how Keneally engages with the past as an Australian writer, is it possible to draw any conclusions of general use in approaching his work? Authors are always at risk here, for while readers who have enjoyed one book will understandably hope to encounter similar qualities in a new one, many readers resent books which fit too neatly into any 'formula', and look to be (moderately) surprised. A cynic might argue that Keneally has handled this dilemma remarkably well, providing variety of character and setting through an impressive panorama of historical material, yet always focusing in close-up (often very cinematically) on those moments of moral crisis in which an individual confronts seemingly timeless decisions of great importance. It is in such apparently intimate glimpses of historical figures that Keneally enthralls us with the sense of 'being there' at the making of history, yet also enables us to understand that only rarely is any of us conscious of 'making history'. Such selection from and structuring of human actions, and especially the attribution of importance to them and their consequences, is traditionally that of the professional historian, to whom Keneally expresses his indebtedness – and whose work his own fictions both resemble and subvert.

In the following chapters some books by Keneally will be discussed in detail with the dual aim of seeking to understand the interest that the subject treated held for the author and of discussing the demands that the text makes upon the reader. Of necessity, this book can only discuss a small selection of Keneally's fiction; he has often published a book a year, and sometimes two. Emphasis is therefore on the identification and analysis of recurrent patterns and preoccupations in Keneally's work rather than on explication of specific texts; not all characters or incidents will be discussed even where a book features quite extensively here. The reader should accept this approach as an invitation to acquire skills in general 'reading' rather than 'information' specifically about Keneally, his life or his work.

Keneally's own approach to the business of writing stresses craft rather than any concept of God-given gift or 'genius', partly as a deliberate counterblast to the claims of academe but partly, also, because he seems to believe quite genuinely that the role and function of the writer in modern society has changed (or certainly *ought* to change) by comparison with earlier periods. The nature of such a change can only be properly understood in the context of Keneally's own understanding of the contemporary world's relationship with its past, especially so as his fiction is itself mostly concerned with a vivid re-presentation of the past to the present. One effect of a concern with the past, and what meanings we might attribute to it, is almost inevitably a powerful awareness of transience and mortality; the more successfully a writer succeeds in evoking, in 'bringing alive', scenes and personalities from earlier periods (and this is something that Keneally certainly devotes much time and invention to doing) then the more must the reader be aware of their simultaneous presence and absence, as it were. So near, and yet so far, a past created in all its 'reek and savour' makes us disturbingly aware of the presentness of the period; it also – no less disturbingly – reminds us that our own present will be someone else's past, and will therefore be subject to the same speculations, shapings and misreadings as we are guilty of in looking back from our vantage point.

2

Figures in a National Landscape: *Bring Larks and Heroes* and *Three Cheers for the Paraclete*

It is curious that Australians have always favoured that species of hero who goes down inevitably against outlandish odds but who does it with style. This expectation of failure, the stress on elegant courage, is something the Australians have taken directly from the Irish character.
(Thomas Keneally, *Beyond the Dreamtime*)

'Damn it all, it's good for a man to be uncertain. Certainty's only a front-end of a beast whose backside is bigotry.'
(*Three Cheers for the Paraclete*)

Keneally established his reputation both nationally and internationally with the publication in 1967 and 1968 of two prize-winning books set in Australia which, though depicting very different periods (the 1790s and the late 1960s) and ostensibly exploring very different issues, complement each other in their plotting of individual against larger destinies: *Bring Larks and Heroes* (1967) and *Three Cheers for the Paraclete* (1968).

Bring Larks and Heroes is regarded within Australian literature as a classic exploration of the early days of Keneally's own country, not so much for its description of physical location (which is sparse) as for the moral and spiritual awareness with which it invests the day-to-day life of convict society. Robert Hughes, reviewing the book in 1968, hailed Keneally as 'the first novelist to use Australia's past intelligently', despite passages where he appears as a 'natural writer trying to be unnatural and floundering in Catholicized rhetoric'.[1] Nowhere is Keneally's religious cast of imagination better revealed than in the way he seeks to understand the early settler past of his own country. It is a past whose extremes of heroism and suffering appeal strongly and productively to his imagination, the more so because the very founding of Australia as a British penal colony in 1788 contained deep moral and existential contradictions unparalleled elsewhere. Comparison with the founding of America may seem appropriate, but there could be no greater difference between the high-minded principles which inspired the Founding Fathers to cross the Atlantic and the still-disputed mix of strategic interests, commercial considerations and pressing social needs which led to the eleven vessels of the First Fleet sailing from Portsmouth in May 1787 with their 'cargo' of some 580 male and 190 female convicts. Indeed, one likely reason for the establishment of a penal colony in Australia was that the 1775–81 War of Independence had closed America as a destination for British convicts. The bizarre juxtapositions constituted by this mixed settlement fleet of officers, seamen and convicts, whose task was to found a self-sufficient community which would function also as a prison, not only appealed to Keneally's novelistic imagination but have also left their mark on the Australian nation's own myths of national identity:

> There is a fascination inherent in the question of who these people were, these Australian first-comers, these fallen Adams and Eves, their crimes written on their foreheads and in their eyes and emphasised by their chains.
> (*Beyond the Dreamtime*, 18)

Of course, the fascination that Keneally describes as 'inherent' in the 'question' of these people is actually inherent in *his* fascination with the period (it is he who sees the 'first-comers' as 'fallen Adams and Eves'); even in this critical comment Keneally demonstrates his adeptness at shifting from personal opinion to ostensible fact.

Bring Larks and Heroes can also usefully be seen as a late-sixties response, albeit removed in time and place, to the moral and military conflicts in which Australia became embroiled through supporting the United States in Vietnam; the dilemma of largely innocent individuals caught in dangerous power-play larger than themselves is as

---

1. Robert Hughes, 'Conscience and the corporal', *Times Saturday Review*, 24 February 1968, p.21.

central to Keneally's depiction of settlement Australia as to national debate between 1965 and 1972. In an important complementary sense 'Keneally's central concern . . . is with the need of the individual to seek salvation *within society*.[2]

If the first reluctant settlers in Australia were 'fallen Adams and Eves', the role allotted in the new historical era to Australia's Aboriginal inhabitants, whose nomadic use of the land had continued uninterrupted for at least 50,000 years, was decidedly less central. It was impossible for the two cultures to understand one another, especially on the crucial question of land use or ownership, and relations soured rapidly to a state of savage, prolonged – and very unequal – warfare. The Aborigines were often ruthlessly exploited, even casually murdered; their position was little better than that of slaves in their own country. Not until the mid 1960s did some Aboriginals even receive the recognition of being counted in the official Census, and the right to vote.

The harsh realities of the convict settlement and the more enduring wrongs suffered by generations of Aboriginal peoples provide the fabric of these two books by Keneally. Both works treat themes which will inevitably be viewed very differently by Australians (and by different groups of Australians) and non-Australians, and this question of Keneally's status as novelist or as *Australian* novelist will be addressed in the Conclusion of this study. Suffice here to say that in both books an Australian writer engages with historical material which evokes deeply-felt responses, and has in some respects proved controversial. Remembering the cultural climate in which Keneally grew up, his boldness in tackling these subjects is undoubted, and his own writings have in turn contributed to a growing desire to reappraise aspects of Australian history often skirted around in earlier periods. In these ways a writer of fiction can have a considerable impact upon ways in which a society views itself, and its past.

Keneally records in his Author's Note to *Bring Larks and Heroes* that 'the germ-idea' for the novel grew from a passage in the journal *A Complete Account of the Settlement at Port Jackson in New South Wales*' (1793) by Captain Watkin Tench (c.1758–1833), and emphasises that 'The geography of the colony suggests that of Sydney, but is not meant to be identified with it'. He also asks the reader to accept that 'the world of this novel is a world of its own'. The two comments point up Keneally's approach to his imaginative

---

2. Brian Kiernan, 'Thomas Keneally and the Australian Novel: A Study of *Bring Larks and Heroes*', *Southerly*, 28/3 1968, pp.189–99. Reference on p.199.

rendering of history, and usefully steer the reader away from any temptation to read the book too closely as a detailed 'costume drama' with a specific setting – through the reference to Tench's account makes clear that the 'germ' of the idea lay in the close geographical correspondence between that early written record of the infant colony and Keneally's own life, past and present, in the Sydney area. He has also described the book as a 'personal exorcism' in which he 'tried to look at universal moral issues in terms of our early history'.

The opening of *Bring Larks and Heroes* exemplifies that cinematic immediacy with which Keneally brings history alive through apparently informal, but in fact carefully contrived, specific detail:

> At the world's worse end, it is Sunday afternoon in February. Through the edge of the forest a soldier moves without any idea that he's caught in a mesh of sunlight and shade. Corporal Halloran's this fellow's name. He's a lean boy taking long strides through the Sabbath heat.

Also typical is the use of authorial comment, here deliberately intrusive and contradictory of any easy suspension of disbelief: 'Visibly, he has the illusion of knowing where he's going. Let us say, without conceit, that if any of his ideas on this subject were *not* illusion, there would be no story.' The effect of this opening is to point up a divergence between options apparently available to the characters (their 'illusion' of knowing where they are going), and a wider pattern of destiny in terms of which they are already 'caught in a mesh' whose strands are as yet invisible; when these are revealed, as they are eventually to Halloran, it is too late. The novel will close with his death-throes on the gallows. For the reader, the 'mesh of sunlight and shade' within which the lone figure moves brings also suggests the shaping hand of the author in this account, as well as hinting at an unseen pattern in our own present-day activities.

Keneally displays an enduring preoccupation with events which may be the stuff of history, or may prove historically insignificant even while (for those involved) literally matters of life and death. Halloran is an innocent in a dangerously fallen world, and his acquisition of knowledge brings not only pain but the destruction of Ann, his 'secret bride . . . in Christ', and himself (as a soldier he cannot reveal his relationship with the convict Ann). Such harsh workings of fate can be handled with a spare economy by Keneally in the strictly contrived setting he chooses for their unravelling, a setting also contrived quite deliberately at the time to achieve certain mixed social and strategic objectives. The book contains scenes of nauseating physical suffering and torment along with examples of spiritual strength and unselfish affection; illustrations of mankind's innate capability for outright turpitude and for exemplary goodness. It would be a complacent reader who believed that today's more 'civilized' society had outgrown the disturbing elements of this behaviour (any more than it had excelled the finer gestures), and Keneally's point is precisely that in such matters little changes through the centuries. But the particular historical setting chosen does allow him to emphasise the brutality of the mortal bounds to human moral and spiritual aspirations. He frequently stresses the effects on the inmates of the crude recreation of English social structures in that eighteenth-century Australia, 'the human sink in which we serve our King . . . this small parish of hell' (Ch.1).

Given such daunting physical constraints, the romantic element in *Bring Larks and Heroes*, the mutual love – and eventual mutual destruction – of Phelim Halloran and Ann Rush, can be no sentimental romp. Here too, though, Keneally is more interested in establishing that the shadow under which the two lovers play out their parts falls not only across the shores of colonial Australia but is one under which we all live out our mortal lives. From the start Halloran's love for his 'secret bride' is shot through with a darker awareness of the fragility of happiness: 'A long acrid pity for an Ann who would weep, bleed and perish in season, possessed him most of his days' (Ch.1). Like T.S. Eliot's vision of the dramatist John Webster, who 'saw the skull beneath the skin', Halloran is only too aware in embracing Ann of 'the skull-case, dear and mortal, beneath her hair'. For the reader, such phrases echo the 'mesh of sunlight and shade' in which we first saw Halloran himself, and with hindsight can be interpreted as foreshadowing the tragic end of the lovers' relationship. But if Halloran's moral attitude to the physical aspects of love is determined by his strict religious upbringing, he is also a total innocent in understanding his physical relationship with Ann for what it is, and in taking 'precautions' against her pregnancy: 'He had no sisters, or rather, they had both died in childhood. To him a woman functioned by laws of pythagorean grandeur and white rules of sacrilege. He was willing to be serene on medical grounds about the red cord, that it would protect Ann' (Ch.4). For her part, she sees his sensitivity and innocence as 'not made for the way of things' (Ch.10), a view confirmed in a later authorial comment (with reference to a planned robbery from the stores): 'Halloran needed to believe that the plan had dropped whole and mandatory from heaven, that it was woven all of a piece. He could not be permitted to see the thing customarily put together out of oddments' (Ch.21). Such innocence, not to say naivety, is in Ann's eyes part of Phelim's

endearing vulnerability; under the wider mesh of destiny cast by the
novel his innocence will cost them both dearly.

In his simple-minded, if wholly admirable, framework of belief
and action, Halloran can be seen as doomed in the penal colony of
Australia, 'a fearful lonely place' in which he and his fellows are 'lost
in the dark on the scruff of the world' (Ch.16). The limited nature
of the options open to individuals such as Halloran or Ann sharpens
the ruthlessness of their end; Ann may protest to Byrne that 'There's
always a choice', but his reply denies all hope: 'If there is, how did
you end in this town?' (Ch.21). Against Halloran's trusting simplicities
Keneally sets the shrewd optimism of Hearn, who seeks to turn the
optimistic pretensions of the early settlement to his own advantage
by stealing the promissory notes and sailing to South America:

> And you must remember, this little town of ours was meant to be a
> Corinth of the south, as they say. The consul in Valparaiso wouldn't
> be surprised to see a note signed by His Excellency for an amount
> within the bounds of reason. (Ch.22)

There is a sense here of tragi-comic melodrama, of individuals and
nations acting out parts which are ill-written and ill-suited; this image
Keneally was to use explicitly in *The Playmaker* (1987) twenty years
later, a novel which was appropriately itself the basis for a successful
play in 1988 (*Our Country's Good* by Timberlake Wertenbaker).

A sharp poignancy is given to individual expressions of kindness and
affection within this novel by Keneally's unremitting description of the
physical suffering inflicted by the convict system. The parameters of
the torture, whether physical or mental, that human beings are capable
of inflicting on one another has always interested him, and the penal
colony of Australia (like Nazi Germany or the modern conflict in
Eritrea) demands that the writer confront such matters:

> Given the place that the convict occupies in Australian myth, we
> were always of course quite willing to believe the worst of them,
> and over the penal period in Australia both the most remarkable
> of visionaries and the most pitiable of sadists would find a place
> for themselves. . . . The rule Australia imposed on everyone from the
> start was that you had to take it on its own terms, and they were
> very individual terms.
> (Thomas Keneally, *Beyond the Dreamtime*, 22)

Violence played a unique role in Australia's early history, for it was
an essential aspect of the colony's role as a penal institution, a central

and formal part of the society itself – no matter how much the young colony might aspire to be the new 'Corinth of the south'. The horrors of transportation are especially keenly felt by Irish Australians; the great majority of the convicts were Irish, and the continuing 'Troubles' in Northern Ireland today echo old injustices (the eighteenth-century English authorities were only too ready to ship the troublesome Irish – as they saw them – to the distant prison settlement). Bishop Costello in *Three Cheers for the Paraclete* gives passionate expression to this vision of the Catholic faith in Australia:

> The price we have paid throughout the centuries for this faith! . . . The price we have paid here! Our first priest a convict, political prisoner, shipped for months in a reeking hold, beaten in prison three hundred times with a wire cat [whip]. (Ch.12)

In *Bring Larks and Heroes* there is constant emphasis upon physical suffering and the weakness of the flesh, and Keneally spares us no detail. The horrors of the human body in agony or in decomposition also evoke for him what seems a deeply ambivalent response to sexual pleasure, and in this he echoes many traditional Christian teachings. In Chapter 6, Halloran has cause to visit Surgeon Daker's hospital, and amid 'a melee of bodies and ills' is confronted by a scene of intercourse between a blind woman and an orderly; 'They were people, even separately, ugly beyond telling. A preacher like John Chrysostom would have delighted to have them mate beneath his pulpit as he preached on the viciousness of the flesh, on the death-sweat and -bed of love.' The reference to St John Chrysostom (c.345–407) can be attributed to Halloran's own upbringing, but the same revulsion recurs in Keneally's work, often accompanied – as here – by description of the extent to which man is 'tethered unto damnation by his . . . body' (Ch.16). The possibility of incarnation conflicts with the actuality of mankind's sexual appetites, as Halloran is only too aware. He is excited by the scene in spite of himself, and in seeking to capture the grotesqueness of *his* emotion in this situation, the text itself lapses into the grotesque: 'lust, the size of a hippopotamus, flopped over in the tropic swamps of Halloran's belly. Oh, it alarmed him to have his bowels yearn out towards that sort of oblivion' (Ch.6). Such sexual oblivion, here rendered in overly physical terms, is to be both contrasted and compared with Halloran's fear of final 'oblivion' for himself and Ann on the scaffold: 'the death of man, stinking, apoplectic, pop-eyed . . . More than hell, he feared to have her jerking in the full, uninformed terror of strangling' (Ch.27).

As a soldier, Halloran's own position within the brutal convict system is deeply ambiguous, as Hearn takes delight in pointing out: 'more than honest, you're conscience-bound. . . . You're afraid of this system you guard with your strong young arm. You are not afraid of its noose and knout [whip], but of how it stands to your conscience' (Ch.11). The Jesuit poet Gerard Manley Hopkins (1844–89) understood well that the mind, too, 'has mountains; cliffs of fall', and Keneally's work often centres upon such inner conflict, compared with which physical terrors are more easily borne. The thinking soldier, whether Joan of Arc (in *Blood Red, Sister Rose*) or General Sherman (in *Confederates*) is the perfect figure to grapple with the potentially contradictory demands of conscience and of military expediency. Such conflicts assume special proportions for an individual who is also a priest (as in Keneally's next novel, *Three Cheers for the Paraclete*), but they confront all human beings who strive, often against the odds, to discern order in life. The military responsibilities of a soldier are directly geared to the destruction of life, even through action undertaken in obedience to orders, and Keneally renders such moments of professional killing as horrendous for their fascination with technical detail – the cold curiosity of discovery on the part of the inexpert killer – as for the act of killing itself. This theme was to receive extended treatment in *The Chant of Jimmie Blacksmith*, but in *Bring Larks and Heroes* it is Byrne who has to bayonet a convict who has rebelled:

> The bayonet gestured softly at the boy, who turned his back and took it in the buttocks. . . . The iron went into his belly, high up because he was rolling; and he was so close to death . . . Byrne was enthralled by the barbarous fluidity of his bayonet going in. He actually felt for the man's softer parts with his boot and spiked him a last time. (Ch.15)

To acquire such horrific knowledge is also human, but Keneally's book seeks to clarify both the pressures and confusions which might demand such dreadful learning. As Brian Kiernan has observed, 'The novel probes life at its extremes; but fundamental to its form is that Halloran and Ann represent the possibilities of life, and social life, unattainable in such a denatured society.'[3] Another Australian commentator on Keneally has seen the portrait of Phelim in *Bring Larks and Heroes* as 'One of the happiest outcomes of Keneally's need to use himself as an authorised source of information' – an

---

3. Ibid.

issue to which we shall return elsewhere in this book – suggesting that 'he has broken no new ground in characterisation' because 'he is not interested in being informed by the world beyond himself.'[4] Keneally himself has commented in correspondence that the book 'isn't even a novel. It's a prose work, grotesquely overesteemed'; he claimed that *Three Cheers for the Paraclete*, to which we turn next, was 'more genuinely and honestly a novel in the novel tradition than *Bring Larks and Heroes*'.[5] The author's harsh judgement of this early work seems uncalled for; there are fine passages in the novel reflecting human warmth and humour, while on the other side the book charts all too clearly the consequences for human relationships, let alone for salvation, of mankind's enduring inhumanity to man.

Bring Larks and Heroes explored issues always with us, but through the recreation of events from a distant period; for non-Australians events distant in place as well as time. In *Three Cheers for the Paraclete*, Keneally addressed his talents to the problems of individual and professional faith in following the dilemmas of a trainee priest in contemporary Sydney, a story which echoes Keneally's own planned future before his change of mind late in the day. He has described it as 'a novel of organisational politics' (a reference to the 'corporation' of the Catholic church) which in its tensions reflected at the time 'the stage innumerable men of good faith are at'.[6] There is always the danger of reading too much of a novelist's life into the fiction: in one sense, it is the fiction alone which properly concerns the reader; the rest is curiosity. It seems perverse, though, not to consider the extent to which *Three Cheers for the Paraclete*, which charts the trials of conscience and temper endured by a young trainee priest who is also secretly an author, might illuminate Keneally's attitudes to such matters. The cover blurb for the early novels drew attention to this very aspect of his life: 'Thomas Keneally was educated in Sydney. He trained for several years for the Catholic priesthood but did not take Orders.' Such references were dropped (somewhat surprisingly, given the book's subject matter) with the publication of *Blood Red, Sister Rose* in 1974. They have since reappeared.

4. David English, 'History and the Refuge of Art: Thomas Keneally's Sense of the Past', *Meridian*, 6/1, May 1987, pp.23–29. Reference on p.24. This short article is the best introduction to this crucial topic; I am greatly indebted to David English's insights in my own discussions here.
5. Thomas Keneally, letter to Brian Kiernan dated 24 October, 1968. MSS Collections, National Library of Australia, Canberra. NLA No. 7017. Folder 1.
6. Ibid.

Father Maitland, the trainee priest whose struggles with conscience and with authority we follow in *Three Cheers for the Paraclete*, may be seen in retrospect as very much a spiritual child of the late sixties. In the Europe from which he has just returned, 1968 was – as in the United States – a milestone year of student revolt against authoritarian structures in education and society, and it seems no coincidence that Maitland's subversive theological study has been published during the time he spent in Belgium. To what extent Keneally himself (who was 33 when the novel was published) felt affected by such movements of the time is uncertain, but the novel centres upon the conflict for Maitland between individual thought and the received wisdom of ecclesiastical tradition. In personal terms this is also a clash between his views as a trainee priest and an older generation of priests who have almost complete say over his daily life in the seminary. The parallels with military life are clear.

His instinctive friendliness and wit, together with his occasional fits of temper, give Maitland considerable appeal; he might be seen as a hero, but the complexity of the story's ending stresses the priestly (rather than 'heroic') virtues of patient service and self-effacement. Against such admirable and essentially human qualities Keneally pits others, equally human but less admirable, notably the hierarchical arrogance of the priesthood career structure. The very title of the book derives from the scene in Chapter 12 where the appointment of Costello as a bishop is announced in the seminary and Maitland, whose opinion of Costello is decidedly mixed, remarks acidly to a fellow trainee: 'Three cheers for the Paraclete'. The term 'Paraclete' itself comes from a Greek word meaning advocate, intercessor, or comforter, and as a title of the Holy Spirit is often used in the sense of 'the Comforter', as in John 14:16, where Jesus says to his distraught disciples, shortly before his arrest and crucifixion: 'And I will pray the Father, and he shall give you another Comforter, that he may abide with you for ever.' Much of the sharpest (and wittiest) criticism of the church offered in Keneally's book is aimed at those aspects of priestly procedure and authority which, to Maitland's way of thinking, run directly counter to such Christian love and humility.

The most rewarding reading of Keneally's early books is one alert to themes which recur in his later writing, albeit in subtly-changing ways. Under this aspect *Three Cheers for the Paraclete* also exemplifies that lasting concern with the Christian paradox of the Incarnation in which, as the visionary poet William Blake (1757–1827) expressed it at about the time of Australia's settlement in 1788, 'God becomes as we are that we may be as he is'. This paradox has already been noted in *Bring Larks and Heroes*. As a trainee priest (committed to certain ideals, but not yet confirmed in them) Maitland embodies and articulates those loves, hates and frustrations which occupy much of our time, but from which we fondly believe priests to be exempt. The greater part of the paradox for Keneally is that, with all their foibles and failings, priests really *do* have the power of special access and intercession in moments of greatest human suffering. The unexpected resolution of the book, in terms not of individual choice but of communal work and shared faith, reaffirms a stance towards life unsurprising for a believer, but as challenging for most readers today as it must have been in 1968. However tempted we may be to see something of Keneally's own failings (as well as faith) in Maitland, the central fact is that the latter opts for that priestly life which Keneally himself rejected in order to become the writer whose book we read. The relation between biography and fiction here is no simple mirroring of personal experience, rather one of symbiotic complexity.

Strong in many of Keneally's books is a desire to evoke the special loneliness and vulnerability of those in positions of moral responsibility. Here, too, the calling of the priesthood operates as more than a specific example; it is a model, a paradigm, of the tangled web of hopes, fears and beliefs which carry us (with greater or lesser success) through each day, and which bind us inexorably to the lives of others. The opening paragraph of *Three Cheers for the Paraclete*, in which Maitland is celebrating an open-air Mass for a guild of graduates on a headland near the city, captures a sense of youthful pleasure and priestly isolation:

> They reclined on rugs and ground-sheets as if they might well be preparing to drink coffee or make love. This somehow gave him the sense that what he performed had an affinity to the earth and the elements and the blood. So that, for the first time since coming home at Christmas, he did not feel an alien.

In such situations the role of women, and of sexual desire, is often uncertain in Keneally's writings, and Maitland's initial reaction in this scene to his cousin's wife reflects a poignant tension between sensual beauty and religious propriety: 'She seemed irradicably old-world and knew her place before a priest. As well, she was appallingly lovely.'

The early contradictions in this passage between formal structures and individual response, the head and the heart, prefigure the larger conflicts of the novel. Relevant, too, is the passing reference to Maitland's recent return from Europe, for just as in *Bring Larks and Heroes* the tragedy unfolded in a colony whose wider future was controlled from afar, so in this book the distant but ever-present authority of the Vatican is the context against which more local disputes unfold. In both cases, Europe represents both a controlling power and a greater freedom (the French Revolution in *Bring Larks and Heroes*, a liberal publishing house here) with which the special trials of life in Australia are contrasted. There is a tradition of such physical and spiritual suffering in Australian literature, not least because of the actual hardship of early exploration and settlement, the most extensive example being Henry Handel Richardson's trilogy *The Fortunes of Richard Mahony* (1930); more recently, Patrick White's novel *Voss* (1957) explored the thesis that 'true knowledge comes from death by torture in the country of the mind'. Peter Carey's *Oscar and Lucinda* (1988) exemplifies a knowing, post-modern, handling of the tradition (especially in Oscar's eventual suffering and death).

A feature shared by such texts, as by many Australian films of the seventies, was a preoccupation with landscape, but Keneally's fiction departs from this tradition in its focus upon an inner conflict unrelated to 'landscape' elements. In these two early books the brief glimpses of landscape add little to a drama essentially intellectual and emotional. Disjunction between everyday life and the complex mix of memories and expectations we bring to it enables Keneally to explore issues of perennial concern through characters and events whose supposed ordinariness is often their most striking characteristic. Conversely, he rarely misses the chance to stress the all too human characteristics of famous 'historical' figures (Joan of Arc, for example). His particular blend of seriousness and humour, of scholarly significance and pointed informality, recalls the deliberately startling techniques employed by the seventeenth-century 'metaphysical' poets in works which brought together divine and profane passions. For Keneally the novelist, the inherent contradictions of humanity are of inexhaustible interest; maybe Keneally the trainee priest found them more than his calling could accommodate.

St Peter's House of Study, in which Maitland is pursuing his training, embodies everything inimical to the pleasures of this world: 'a grotesque stone bulk' of a boarding school, which has become the 'cavernous symbol of his unhappiness' (Ch.1). As readers we first encounter the House and its administrators in the context of Maitland secretly accommodating his cousin (and his beautiful wife) overnight, when they find themselves without anywhere to stay. The contrast between the central Christian image of shelter and the outraged sensibilities of Monsignor Nolan – 'This has been a celibate house since its foundations were laid' (Ch.1) – indicates precisely the nature of the conflict that is to inform the book:

> The cold fust of old books assailed him in the dark; devotional books, Dublin 1913, a good year for the unalloyed faith. Why couldn't he have been alive and priested then? Saving up indulgences, averting tumours of the throat with a St Blaise candle, uttering arcane litanies; going off to the holocaust the following year to be outraged at the intemperate use of the Holy Name by the men in the trenches; dying in 1924 of dropsy, rosaries, and the certainty of Paradise'. (Ch.1)

Such wry (mental) invective makes Maitland an attractive figure as a secret and subversive author, appealing to all those who question the symbols and structures of authority. For him, as for many devout Christian priests worldwide (but increasingly now for those in the Third World), an added complication is that his priestly duty often appears to demand just such questioning of his superiors.

The book that Maitland had published under the name of Quinlan in Belgium was entitled *The Meanings of God*, and 'was intended to be a historical study, even if it did not permit the same type of ordered treatment as would a life of Garibaldi or Lola Montez'. As he saw it, if 'there was a difference between what God was and what man, at this or that stage, thought God was, then this was a work of history and not of theology' (Ch.4). Back in Australia, Maitland finds himself in the bizarre situation of being asked to assess this supposedly heretical text: 'On one level it was impossible not to be gratified as a schoolboy' (Ch.4). Such images of childlike simplicity – and oversimplification – recur in the scene where Maitland is asked formally by his bishop to attack the text, and declines. Keneally closes the fraught (and, for the reader, entertaining) encounter with a scene which explicitly seeks to establish the timelessness of the issues involved:

> In the long distempered room, near the wide fireplace, gobs of light from the chandelier resting with the tranquillity of drowned moons on the habitually polished table, he looked like the Bishop of Artois or Autun on a cold night in a Balzac novel. It begged an act of faith to believe that [outside] acquisitive fires of neon splashed the avenues and jackhammers barked on flood-lit construction sites. (Ch.7)

Significantly, too, His Grace stresses that Maitland's scholarship (which Maitland himself thinks might just enable a layman 'to teach history to senior boys') belongs not to him, but to the Church: 'if there was ever a question of obedience, it would belong to me or my successor more than yourself. Remember that and your safety is assured' (Ch.7).

This world of impersonal scholarship, obedience and Christian faith is contrasted with Maitland's journey to visit his cousin, Joe Quinlan, to whom he gives the royalty cheque from *The Meanings of God*. The Quinlans live in a characterless suburb which can be seen as the epitome of that period of uncaring housing development that Patrick White tellingly named 'Barranugli' in his 1961 novel *Riders in the Chariot*:

> Outside an empty supermarket stood the right bus. Rolling off at last, it showed him all the things he could have predicted. Down flat streets jury-masted with power poles, the bus was hailed by neanderthal wives near phone-booths, joyless service-stations, abject corner shops.
> He got out at a street of plaster-board houses. (Ch.8)

The tone of this passage captures something of the despair we may all have felt at some time, in some place, when confronted with the chaos (at best, the anonymity) of much modern urban 'planning'. It is unclear, though, to what extent Keneally expects the reader to accept such dismissive judgements as his own, or those of Maitland, though later he shows the bitterness of the latter to stem from the very heart of his priestly calling:

> 'Would you like a cup of tea, father?' she [Mrs Quinlan] said. Suddenly the old flesh-hatred of his youth turned his stomach and he was aware of what the inconsolable sacrifice was – to live in plaster-board with such a woman.
> 'It's all right, Morna,' he told her urgently, and took improper comfort in knowing that he would be home in Nolan's house by seven. (Ch.8)

Keneally here suggests the motives which took Maitland into the priesthood originally, while returning us to the essentially mysterious yet mundane nature of incarnation: if mankind is indeed made in God's image, then this image includes the 'neanderthal wives' at the bus-stop, Morna not least. To such a challenge, Maitland's only answer at this stage is flight; Keneally's more complex reaction is expressed in the novel overall.

An important dimension of ordinary human community conspicuously lacking in Maitland's life is female company (though any 'flesh hatred' excludes the 'appallingly lovely' Greta). Keneally demonstrates a deep fascination with the ambiguities of bonding in completely or largely one-sex communities: his early book *The Place at Whitton* (1964) – also set in a seminary – is an early example. The alternatives to domestic and married life produced by such communities are sketched in describing Maitland's evenings for students at St John's:

> Gaiety brews easily among monks, soldiers and all other cloistered men. Maitland had only to make it clear that they were his guests, to move the radiator closer, to produce the yellow cake-tin with its picture of the King of the Belgians, to set the odd brotherhood of his four cups ready for coffee, and these mechanical and graceless acts assured the success of the evening. (Ch.9)

There is deliberate but ironic evocation here of the ceremony of Mass, and of the mystery of transubstantiation; the contents of the 'yellow cake-tin', and the setting out of the four unmatched cups, ensures the success of the evening because those who come believe in that success. The wanting and the finding derive from the same informing belief, and Maitland finds this both pathetic and disturbing precisely because he lacks such certainty of belief himself. When a fellow trainee-priest confronts him with a woman who has arrived one evening, Maitland's unease – that unease we encounter elsewhere in Keneally's writings – is only too evident:

> Carrying the woman was what sobered Maitland. . . . As a youth he had taught himself and had been taught a series of celibate's tricks and had learnt them too well. Now he found it easy to remember that this woman shared her species with Morna Quinlan, was mortal and menstrual, and would distend with child and decline with child-bearing. He found it too easy to remember that whoever had her had a season's fruit. Thinking so had generations of celibates succeeded at their trade. Yet Maitland knew that if he wanted the vision of God he must arrive at a more substantial purity than what was provided by these ploys of mental focus. (Ch.9)

Some might feel that Maitland's questioning vision here also typifies Keneally's own position as author and as former trainee priest. Certainly there are few examples in his work of couples happily married (though he is so himself), and women are frequently presented – as here, albeit in Maitland's jaundiced vision – as threatening creatures whose 'mortal and menstrual' qualities at best impair the purity of spiritual vision, at worst drag man into a mire of sex. Such negative definitions of the female role often come from characters to whose shortcomings the reader has been alerted, and Keneally can thus properly disclaim responsibility for them. On the other hand, there is often little to counterbalance such a negative view; the lingering impression is thus indeed a negative one.

The dynamic of this novel, unlike the workings of the plot, in *Bring Larks and Heroes*, is centred in exactly such inner and moral conflicts. The drama that unfolds is one that demands real and challenging decisions on the part of Maitland, but they are decisions which affect only him and to which the rest of society is supremely indifferent. Keneally stresses the minority of one in which Maitland feels himself to be as a trainee priest, an isolation exacerbated, of course, by the fact that he is also in conflict with the principles and hierarchy of the Church itself. On the final page of the book Maitland casts his dilemma bitterly in terms which juxtapose, but do not resolve, the message of the parables and of modern consumerism:

> He dreaded the iron realities of a priesthood which three out of four men did not believe in, but which he could not forbear believing in. He was the unwise virgin of the modern advertisement, bound to the use of the non-majority soap.

It is revealing that Maitland sees himself, in his isolation and near despair, as a modern version of the unwise virgin in the parable, for in this book especially, though elsewhere in Keneally's writings also, the female character represents everything to be feared as wayward and disruptive of the best-laid plans of men. In the scene in which Maitland, Dr Costello and Monsignor Fleming question a young nun who is 'apparently a little unorthodox' several contradictory strands of the novel come together. As the all-male panel of enquiry prepare to question her, 'knowing that theology was a man's world and that here were men enough for the job', Maitland secretly wishes 'on the poor girl the guts of Joan of Arc, the wit of Heloise' (Ch.11). When the young nun appears, Maitland is delighted by her shrewdness in dialogue as much as by her instinct for what he sees as inexact truth, rather than dry casuistry. However, the terms in which he inwardly formulates his approval are stereotypical, no matter how affirmative Keneally may intend them to be (Maitland certainly does): he 'felt pleased with this nun. She underlined one of the few things he knew about women: that they were essentially ungovernable' (Ch.11). When the nun accepts her guilt, Maitland lists her inwardly with other doubters and transgressors – all of them distinct possibilities (like Joan of Arc herself) for the Keneally treatment:

> The nun bowed her head, obviously accepting on it the blame for having spoken inexactly of the deity. Since this same guilt was shared

by Moses, Augustine, John of the Cross, Teresa of Avila, Joan of Arc and an army of other master [sic] spirits, Maitland hoped she was proud of her crime. She gave no signs, however. (Ch.11)

Three Cheers for the Paraclete is a flawed but revealing novel; it sets out very clearly, even somewhat woodenly, issues of vision and obedience, desire and guilt, which Keneally has explored, under various historical guises, in all his subsequent work. He himself wrote to Brian Kiernan at the University of Sydney in 1968: 'I hope, if ever you're professor of Aust. lit., if you *have* to make them read anything, make it *Paraclete*. It's for real.'[7]

7. Ibid.

3

'A ringside seat to history!':
The Chant of Jimmie Blacksmith

There is in Australian writing only one novel which examines the impact of the two cultures from within an aboriginal mind, and this is my own *The Chant of Jimmie Blacksmith*. . . . I have been assured by Aborigines that this book, despite some errors of detail, is the most informative literary work on the impact between the two cultures as it seen by Aboriginals. . . .
(Thomas Keneally, 'My Fiction and the Aboriginal', 1982)

How, then, do we deal with the Aboriginal dead? White Australians frequently say 'all that' should be forgotten. But it will not be. Black memories are too deeply, too recently scarred. And forgetfulness is a strange prescription coming from a community which has revered the fallen warrior and emblazoned the phrase 'Lest We Forget' on monuments throughout the land.
(Henry Reynolds, *The Other Side of the Frontier: Aboriginal resistance to the European invasion of Australia*, 1981)

If a . . . Thomas Keneally . . . decides to write about Aborigines, after they have done with them, they are discarded. The fringe after all is but a subject for their literary skills, it is not the reality which confronts them every day. They belong to another reality and stand outside looking into the fringe camps inhabited by the Aboriginal writer.
(Mudrooroo Narogin, *Writing from the Fringe*, 1990)

First published in 1972, *The Chant of Jimmie Blacksmith* attracted considerable critical debate through its forthright treatment of interracial sex, and also for the violent scene in which the half-blood Jimmie

murders white women and children with an axe. These qualities were
present also in the 1978 film of the book directed by Fred Schepisi.

Like much of Keneally's work, the book turns on what the cover
blurb for the 1972 Penguin edition terms an 'evocative recreation'
of historical events, in this case a series of actual murders by one
Jimmy Governor which took place in New South Wales in July
1900. Keneally locates the time and place of many events in the
book (including 'recreated' and purely fictional incidents) with what
seems at times a clumsy precision – 'It had been a hot day in December
1898, and Jimmie had felt unease when . . .' (Ch.1) – but the novel
also probes the motives and hopes of individuals acting very much
in the shadow of a history beyond their control. More accurately,
perhaps, in the shadow of 'histories', since the book stresses cultural
diversity and posits alternative historical consciousnesses.

Keneally recognizes the aim of both the historian and the novelist
to cut an ordered path through what Herman Melville evocatively
termed this 'belittered world'. Such shared ground between fiction
and history, not least the need of novelists and historians to tell a story
through the devices of character and plot, may be hotly denied by both
(revealingly, historians can prove very resistant to such suggestions),
but there is much to be gained from transgressing such tidy academic
boundaries. The quality of 'historical fable' which Keneally seeks to
create is illustrated by the opening paragraph of *Jimmie Blacksmith*:

> In June of 1900 Jimmie Blacksmith's maternal uncle Tabidgi –
> Jackie Smolders to the white world – was disturbed to get news
> that Jimmie had married a white girl in the Methodist church at
> Wallah.

The text leads us immediately into character, setting and event, and
we learn that 'Half-breed Jimmie had resulted from a visit some white
man had made to Brentwood blacks' camp in 1878'. On the following
page, though, Keneally obtrudes himself with curious formality, and
announces to the reader: 'It is necessary to take cognizance of Jimmy
[sic] Blacksmith's experience from the day of this initiation to the time
in 1900 that Jackie Smolders went to Wallah' (Ch.1). The book's narrative then operates for six chapters in 'flashback' to give us the story of
Jimmie's mixed parentage and a detailed sketch of his education at the
hands of the Nevilles, a well-meaning but narrow-minded missionary
couple. Narrow-mindedness can require willpower, though, and the
Rev. H.J. Neville himself is not immune to that 'distinctive pull of
some slant-grinned black face' which had produced Jimmie, though
he dutifully (but hardly admirably) remains 'faithful to his dull wife

amidst such cheap, such wantonly appealing black flesh' (Ch.1). Other white men are not so constrained, and nocturnal intimacies between the races are contrasted with the defensive hostility that Jimmie repeatedly encounters from white settlers, not least because he is better educated than many of them; he can read and write.

If Jimmie is a misfit both among his own people and among the settlers who alone can offer employment, his role is rendered more complicated by Keneally's introduction of two international issues for Australians at this time: involvement in the South African War of 1899–1902 and the impending federation of the Australian states into a new nation with its own Parliament in 1901. Jimmie's access to Aboriginal history through tribal customs is counterpointed here, and we learn that the song of an ancient raid which he sings while absconding from the mission school for his initiation ceremonies recounts a woman-stealing that 'had taken place during the English civil war, two and a half centuries before'. Jimmie's tribal memory here predates the very foundation of the white colony in which he finds himself so disadvantaged.

Questions of national identity, and of Australia's relationship with Britain, are complex issues still, and Keneally contrives (at times too obviously) to air these early on by staging an argument between an Australian and an English clerk at a Department of Agriculture office where Jimmie seeks advice on fencing materials. There is sharp irony in the statement that 'It wasn't Jimmie's argument: he wanted a leaflet on what wood should go into fencing', especially in the context of the Englishman's contention that 'there is no such thing as an Australian. The only true Australians are . . . the aborigines' (Ch.1). The Australian clerk in the office is dedicated to tweaking the Englishman's pride, and with him Jimmie establishes the first of many such subservient relationships, allowing himself to be part of the Australian's calculated racial insults. His sense of belonging ironically boosted by such humour, he then:

> ran downstairs laughing, to the street where commercial purpose moved whites up and down the pavements with frowns of dignified intent upon them. Adjusting his face to match this high mood, he stepped out to walk amongst them. (Ch.1)

Jimmie's fantasies of participation in the commercial life of white Australia are rudely destroyed when he is cheated by the first farmer for whom he works. His sense of exclusion stimulates that part-sexual, part-mythical, fascination with the landowner's wife which will later inform his motives for murder:

> What he had done, without understanding it, was to elect her to the stature of ideal landowner's-wife.
> . . .
> He found himself swearing to possess her to depths that were probably not in her.
>   It was strange how she had become inherent to his programme. (Ch.2)

Keneally's stance here is that of the omniscient author, quick to speak directly to the reader, if only for witty purpose. He feels free, for example, to gloss a description of Anglo-Australian antipathies with the authorial quip: 'To say it more clearly, it could make them peevish' (Ch.1). While it is possible here, though, to 'say it more clearly' (if only through the 'intervention' of the supposedly invisible author), when the reader needs to follow the more important relationship between Jimmie and Mrs Healey, Keneally offers only the non-explanatory statement that it was 'strange' how she had become inherent to his 'programme' (a programme at this juncture still unexplained).

   Far from originating in any 'programme', many of Jimmie's actions and attitudes are defensive, adopted without choice in order to retain whatever 'freedom' the various histories he inherits allow him. Loving is more complex even than usual, if not impossible:

> Suspended between the loving tribal life and the European rapture from on high called falling in love (at which even Mr. Neville had hinted), Jimmie Blacksmith held himself firm and soundly despised as many people as he could. (Ch.4)

One person he despises utterly is Senior Constable Farrell, with whom he takes a job as a tracker and general servant, thinking that 'It must be a good reference, to have worked for the police. In a police station he would be fortified against his demanding kinsmen' (Ch.5). Once attired in a soiled and ill-fitting uniform, Jimmie realizes himself to be 'more officially a black now than Tabidgi or [his brother] Mort: a registered, accredited, uniformed blackman; more deeply, more damagingly black than ever' (Ch.5). Farrell proves to be a sadist and sexual pervert, and Jimmie's final task before he leaves is to take down the body of an Aboriginal prisoner who has been sexually abused, then hung, by Farrell. Jimmie has failed again in an attempt to establish a position for himself within the structures of white society, and Farrell's corruption as law officer signifies the institutional corruption of the system he represents.

The repeated setbacks that Jimmie experiences in his relationships with whites make his own character and motivation of central importance for the direction and coherence of the book's narrative. With Jimmie, though, Keneally faces the problem of articulating the motives and sentiments of an inarticulate character who is presented as largely unaware of his own motivation, increasingly so as he is driven to multiple murder. Authorial point of view is not identical to that of Jimmie – we have seen that Keneally comments on events within the narrative – yet lack of clarity in Jimmie's motivation becomes increasingly problematic as the novel progresses, a lack only partly compensated for by the insistent pace with which the narrative follows Jimmie's flight after the murders.

It is to provide an explanatory framework for particular actions that Keneally employs reference to events which, in a conventional historical account, would overshadow the story of Jimmie and his murders. If the looming prospect of federation raises myriad questions about the relationships of Australians to each other, and to the outside world, the involvement of Australian troops in Britain's colonial war in South Africa produces both a counterpoint and a parallel to the local events for which Jimmie is the trigger. As a character remarks later in the book, 'The Boers've got a lot of sympathy ... all they wanted to do was to have their land and keep the black man in his place. Isn't that our policy ... ?' (Ch.10). Many Australians – and others (then and now) – would probably answer 'yes' to this, and against such an all-embracing backdrop Jimmie's aspirations, and the violence their frustration provokes, have a wider relevance, and for Britain (say) as much as for Australia. There is a tension in the novel's workings, though, between Keneally's attempt to tell the story 'from within an aboriginal mind', to make Jimmie a rounded and absorbing character, and his determination to evoke the historical significance of Jimmie's position and actions: 'As Jimmie becomes more real to us, the struggle to engender a sense of the historical moment becomes more intrusive.'[1]

The novel gestures at several points towards such possibilities, first during the office argument when the English clerk rebuts the Australian's assertion that federation has worked in Canada and America: 'didn't the United States have trouble enforcing federation? Would you like a civil war and thousands of dead?' The local boy insists that 'It could never happen here. Can yer imagine Australians

---

1. Helen Daniel, 'Purpose and the Racial Outsider: *Burn* and *The Chant of Jimmie Blacksmith*, *Southerly* 38/1, 1978, pp.25–43. Reference on p.32.

shooting at Australians?' The Englishman argues that those with the best claim to be called 'Australians' – the Aborigines – are the least regarded, to which the prompt reply is 'Jacko? ... He's an honest poor bastard but he's nearly extinct' (Ch.1). Jimmie is ignored by the Australian during this exchange, and the most attention he receives during the novel is when he is being hunted like a dog. Then indeed (white) Australians shoot at (black) Australians, and the small party of settlers seeking to track down Jimmie for themselves draw explicit comparisons between this adventure and the larger conflict for which some of them plan to enlist:

> while squadrons of Mounted Rifles, sent to Dubbo instead of Cape Town, encumbered the west, and parties of volunteers solemnly followed the Blacksmiths' cold spoor, *they* had been only a day behind the devil himself.

> In their night encampments some of them spoke as if the manhunt were a novitiate for the war in South Africa. (Ch.10)

Despite such references, the group's chase after Jimmie and his brother Mort remains a personal quest. For Dowie Stead, the murdered Miss Graf's fiance, the hunt for Jimmie is more deeply personal than the others in the party can even guess at. His desire 'to pay off the black race' has little to do with Jimmie's acts, more with how a 'consumptive black girl called Tessie' brought his father and himself, 'both unbuttoned and grotesquely ready for the same black arse, face to face' in her tent one night (Ch.9). The war in South Africa (for which the Australian papers list many more deaths from enteric fever than at the hands of the Boers) remains, on the other hand, a remote topic of speculation. In the pursuit of Jimmie deaths on both sides are quick and bloody, and all from gunshot wounds – apart from Jimmie's own hanging.

The public execution of Jimmie, with which the book closes, falls at a particularly sensitive time for the new Australian authorities, and Keneally makes much of their need to distance it from the public pomp of federation. Just as Jimmy's story, with its uncomfortable South African parallels, runs counter to any optimistic federation rhetoric, so his execution sits ill with the supposed innocence of the new nation in its 'state of grace, the old crimes done' (Ch.15). As a masonic contact informs the New South Wales public hangman, Mr Wallace Hyberry (who had been in the running for the award of an MBE): 'it'll be hard enough choosing a time to hang 'em. Everyone'll be in such a high frame of mind with all this federation nonsense. Hangin' and things to do with it'll be a little bit out of place' (Ch.12).

Mr Hyberry is a butcher by trade (an invention of Keneally's, though a previous New South Wales hangman had been a poulterer) and the narrative implicitly contrasts the impulsive violence of Jimmie's axe murders with that cold professionalism with which a society executes those it decides should pay the ultimate price. Of such ritualistic and impersonal violence Mr Hyberry is the perfect instrument, and Keneally's deadpan description of his tradesman's 'facilities' alert us to read between, as well as along, the lines:

> In Balmain, a riverside suburb of the city of Sydney, the public hangman for the State of New South Wales kept a scrupulous butchery. There was clean sawdust on the floor each day, a capacious coolroom and two polite sons. He himself was an exemplary man, full of placid love. Three mornings a week he or one of his sons bought carcasses at the Homebush slaughteryards. He was at his most talkative on meat: he would pick up lumps of sirloin and praise their texture before housewives. (Ch.9)

Significantly, the reader first encounters Mr Hyberry's name on the lips of Constable Farrell, who tells Jimmie that he has 'jest took a man t' Wellington t' get hanged', and introduces the 'famous gentleman' Mr Hyberry as a 'butcher from Balmain and public hangman as well. He's a scholar, Mr Hyberry. One of the honours of me life, meeting him' (Ch.5). Farrell's respect for Mr Hyberry's distinctive qualities is shared by the ladies of Balmain, who 'thought he was refined, almost like some of the foreign gentlemen in the hair shops in town' (Ch.9). The hangman is a natural focus for morbid curiosity, as much for the mundane as for the deadly nature of his work: a murderer at least has a motive, the hangman only a part-time government job. Most of Mr Hyberry's neighbours in Balmain simply accept this dual nature of his social role – 'They all knew he was the public hangman and said they couldn't imagine him hanging a soul' – but Keneally allows the possibility of exploring more closely Mr Hyberry's role as a public employee through a necrophilic customer named Ted Knoller, a regular customer the butcher himself 'could have lost without regret' (Ch.9).

On our first meeting with Knoller the shift from Jimmie's murders to the butcher's shop is made (wittily, though arguably not entirely appropriately) through description of events at the Newby farm in the papers that day as a 'shambles' (a word which originally denoted the slaughterhouse bench upon which animals were dismembered).

Knoller (not a man to mince his words) expresses his all-consuming curiosity succinctly:

> Yer don't know the killers, and yer don't know those poor women who got killed. Jimmie Blacksmith's a name yer never heard of. But now yer know yer going t'meet him on the gallows. For the final act in a killing that'll always be remembered. Yer got a ringside seat to history! . . . (Ch.9)

Hyberry's assurance that, on the contrary, he is 'just part of the apparatus' is as chilling in its disclaimer of any emotional involvement in (or responsibility for) the processes of 'justice' as Knoller's appetite for grisly titbits of inside information is nauseating. Leaving aside Keneally's pun over Hyberry never having hung 'a soul' (he only hangs the body), the exchange with Knoller over the slabs of meat – 'it was a pleasure to see Mr Hyberry at work on sirloin' (Ch.9) – raises several issues central to the novel. Knoller – necrophile or not – provides the only opportunity in the book for Keneally to reflect the impact of the Blacksmiths' exploits on the proverbial 'man in the street'. Knoller reads the papers assiduously, and his questionings of the hangman while waiting for his meat reveal something of his own interests and motivation: he learns nothing of Hyberry's feelings (if he has any), nor does the reader.

At a deeper level, Knoller's envy of Hyberry's 'ringside seat to history' highlights that special draw which history (on his own admission) holds for Keneally himself, and which has inspired his creation of a range of characters from diverse parts and pasts of the world, from Joan of Arc to the Holocaust. A defining feature of his work is an attempt to strip away the historical trappings of the past (foreign locations, languages, religions, customs) by 'translating' historical events into an immediately accessible form: important historical personages (whose names appear in all the standard school history books) joke, doze, copulate, fart and otherwise demonstrate their downright ordinariness whilst devoting their energies to ends which (whether noble or despicable) reaffirm their common humanity with the reader. They also commit murders, and hang people they have never met. Hyberry's role as suburban family butcher (not to mention his other life as a local Mason with hopes of an MBE) allies him with tradespeople (and Masons) everywhere in public work – and in secret aspirations.

It could be said that Knoller's circus terminology in referring to 'a ringside seat to history' is more appropriate than might appear (or than the author might wish), for the action-packed world of Keneally's fiction, in which Great Names from History perform dizzying acts of an historical – yet joltingly familiar – nature, is often one of spectacle. We admire the inventiveness, the timing, the coordination with which the members of the troupe perform whilst in the spotlight, but beyond that narrow circle of light we are very conscious of the controlling hand of the ringmaster-author. As David English has observed, 'There is no sense in Keneally's historical novels that any one period is different from another, nor could there be if the past is merely the present (that is, Keneally's present) rendered fabulous'.[2] In its relentless reduction of a multifaceted past to an ever-familiar and violent present Keneally's work, English suggests, 'remains profoundly unoriginal'.

One result of a 'ringside seat' approach to history is that Keneally focuses on vivid representation of the eventful – often the violent and shocking – aspects of history, to the detriment of any sense of ordinary life. Hyberry is apparently the most ordinary character in *Jimmie Blacksmith*, but is in fact extraordinary in every respect, saving his behind-the-counter role as family butcher. Even that aspect of his life is rendered bizarre by the conversations with Knoller, by his disturbing appreciation of dead meat, and by the hinted strangeness of his dutiful sons, who never speak and pretend never even to hear.

Typical of how Keneally renders the mundane unnerving is the apparent deadpan reporting of Jimmie's hanging. This parodies a documentary tone, and reinforces that knowing sense of an undefined abnormality which cloaks Hyberry and his sons: 'Mr Hyberry was away three days in all, and his fine boys could cope with the customers' (Ch.15). Knowing as we do nothing whatsover about his 'fine boys' (the phrase echoes the way Balmain ladies might admiringly describe them) they remain as characterless as the sirloin chops they handle, and this itself renders them anything but ordinary; equally, though, we have no grounds for doubting that they are 'fine'. Keneally is adept at toying in this way with the reader, but, on re-reading the technique obscures rather than enhances better understanding of the characters. Performance is all, and a re-reading offers a repeat performance, nothing more. From their first mention – 'a capacious coolroom and two polite sons' (Ch.9) – to our last glimpse of them dutifully 'coping' these filial paragons remain disembodied and unsettling, but to no clear purpose. It is not even clear whether the tone of voice which describes them is the author's, though it is certainly Keneally who originally lists the sons (along with the coolroom) as among the 'apparatus' of what is ambiguously described as Hyberry's 'scrupulous butchery' (Ch.9).

2. David English, 'History and the Refuge of Art', p.24.

Butchery is a recurrent image in this novel (as in others), and only most obviously in the axe-murders at Newby farm. Keneally posits 'scrupulous butchery' as an appropriate description of Hyberry's activities as public hangman; even Knoller has gleaned some details (ironically from *Truth* and *The Sporting Chronicle*) of how an Aboriginal man 'nearly got his head pulled off' when Hyberry, then still learning his 'craft', calculated 'weight, age, momentum' inexactly (Ch.9). Jimmie learns his own new craft swiftly at the Newby farm, from the first moment when his axe 'mined the deep sinews' of old Mrs Newby's shoulder to the leisure with which he chops Miss Graf 'between hip and the ribs', a blow that 'knocked apart her rib cage and split her hams' (Ch.8). The violence of the scene is powerfully conveyed through matched precision of language (often the terminology of the butcher's block — of carcasses rather than bodies) with intention and action; nowhere better than in the speed with which 'Mr Jimmie Blacksmith rolled on his feet and chopped off the back of the remaining Miss Newby's head'. Typically, the only visible result (to the reader) is that the blade of the axe becomes 'flecked with the strange grey mucus of the brain' (Ch.8).

In such passages the intended mystery is of carcasses revealing what life conceals, workings which only violent death (or the dispassionate knife of surgeon or pathologist) lay bare. Horribly wounded, and 'raucous as a beast' in her death throes, Miss Graf 'unreasonably . . . rose to walk, below apprehending' the extent of her injuries (Ch.8). Such linguistic wit (the pun of 'below apprehending': 'below' in that her roars resemble those of a beast, and 'below' in that her lower body registers, or 'apprehends', the crippling physical injuries even if her will to walk remains strong) is that of Keneally the ringmaster, not Jimmie the performer. For this reason the *effects* of the violence are shocking while the actions themselves remain understandable, and so forgivable. The intended association in the reader's mind (not apparently present in Jimmie's) between repressed sexual desire and 'the split bowl' of Miss Graf's belly (Ch.8) exemplify another recurrent theme in Keneally's work, that between the obvious violence of war and the suggested violence of sexual encounter; in both, though in different ways, individuals are fragmented.

Keneally economically depicts the actions and effects of violence, understanding that it is above all the very humanness of the unthinkable, whether murder or execution (the two blend in Jimmie's own mind during the axe scene), that renders it both monstrous and fascinating. He is less sure, though, in articulating for the reader the complex mix of emotions which lead Jimmie to murder and, more crucially, to kill again; Jimmie himself is inarticulate on the subject. His first assessment of what he has done, undertaken 'amongst the slaughtered Newbys' (Ch.8), is unfocused in ways for which his confused state of mind offers no adequate explanation:

> Though he felt buoyant enough, Jimmie Blacksmith knew that he had become an incurable. He knew in an instant that he must see into his acts the fervid illusions they were based on. He chose therefore to know and not to go mad. At the same time, he must be able to see the four hewn women as culprits, and so the mere beginnings of an agenda of mayhem. Yet to see them fully and without doubt as the first necessary casualties of a war regally undertaken was itself a mad act of the mind. (Ch.8)

This passage contains unresolved ambiguities of expression on Keneally's part which are not lessened by the authorial gloss that Jimmie 'was to spend the rest of his life in tenuous elation and solid desolation between self-knowledge and delirium' (Ch.8).

A later passage does go some way towards illuminating the elation and desolation that Jimmie is subject to: Keneally describes him as being 'in a viable balance between belief and non-belief in the dismembering he had done', though the butcher's imagery of 'dismembering' is balanced by the fact that 'the thorough nature of the punishment he had dealt out continued to soothe and flatter him'. He had, he feels, 'been effective'. In such elated moments as executioner Jimmie is proud of having 'actually manufactured death and howling dark for people who had such pretensions of permanence', though in travelling across the mountains to the Healy farm he also harbours other memories and motives: 'Mrs Healy was worth remembering too, with something like a lover's remembrance. If *that* were a form of madness, then he welcomed it' (Ch.10).

After the murder of the Healy family – mother, child and husband, Jimmie constructs moments of elation for himself through visions of what release his actions might bring:

> he secretly let his mind run in splendid patterns, patterns close to dementia, patterns to besot yourself with . . . All the women of the countryside would be in terror of his name; they would sweat palpable fear. He was a walking rape of women's souls. (Ch.10)

Sex is a disturbing tension throughout the book. Jimmie's own origins as a halfbreed provoke the Rev. Neville (himself no stranger to such temptations) to meditate on the coupling that had produced him: 'The

European who had impregnated giddy Dulcie Blacksmith must have been of a pensive nature; a man who perhaps hated the vice of sleeping with a black woman yet could not master it' (Ch.1). Sexual history here is as personal as it is painful, especially so in the case of sex across the racial divide; this element both strengthens and complicates the comparisons with events in South Africa, which act as counterpoint throughout. The impossibility of Jimmie's situation is reflected in the marriage advice he receives from the Nevilles, who invite him to aspire to eventual invisibility: 'If you could ever find a nice girl off a farm to marry, your children would only be quarter-caste then, and your grandchildren one-eighth caste, scarcely black at all' (Ch.2).

Against this supposedly benevolent vision of his descendants' role in Australian society, Jimmie has to balance the uncomplicated sex he finds among his own people, and the situation well-known to both races whereby white men go to black women, and – most painful to him, given his own mixed blood – that complacent married status of the white farmers' wives; symbols of respectability and property. His first job, with Mr Healy, is with 'One of those harsh, commercially-minded Irishmen with a fat, bleak-eyed young wife to sit by his fire and ponder on the crucifix above it' (Ch.2). It is a stereotypical sketch, and whether it ever fitted a group of the population, as Keneally suggests, is at least questionable. Jimmie's view of things is hardly less over-simplified, if more excusable:

> The Nevilles had succeeded so well as to make Jimmie a snob. In the mind of the true snob there are certain limited criteria to denote the value of a human existence. Jimmie's criteria were: home, hearth, wife, land. Those who possessed these had beatitude unchallengeable. Other men had accidental, random life. Nothing better. (Ch.2)

Jimmie's criteria here of the 'value of human existence' are less those of the snob than of the dispossessed; it is those who profess (from positions of some privilege) to find such criteria too materialistic who might more properly be termed snobs. The suppressed sexual attraction which characters like Mrs Healy or Miss Graf have for Jimmie, an attraction which is the mirror-image of the distaste/appeal black women evoke for their stolid husbands, is here subsumed under the wider title of property. A wife might ponder on the crucifix above the fireplace, but her place is by the hearth, as an essential part of the furniture.

This image of the wife bound by deeds and duties to house and husband, while aspiring – if only in daydream – to some spiritual fulfilment that life might offer is emblematic of Keneally's informing interest in the incarnate potential of the individual. Jimmie's desire for respectable white women is one aspect of his attraction to, and recoil from, the white establishment which controls his life. His one chance of a position in this establishment, albeit a lowly one, is cruelly frustrated when Gilda's baby proves to be not his but that of the Irish cook at the sheep station where he had worked. Significantly, Jimmie's first meeting with his future wife is one at which the cook contrives to humiliate Jimmie:

> 'Oh, I've hurt your feelings, Jimmie,' said the cook with a secondary sort of sympathy that was only a small distance from sarcasm. 'We Europeans are so poor in spirit that the best we can do is laugh at primitive people who, in my experience, always have *something*. God knows what it is, but *something*.' The girl sniffed at the word *something*. Wayward girl that she was, she still thought she had a heritage and that she surpassed Jimmie. (Ch.6)

The pregnancy of Jimmie's wife provokes the Newby womenfolk to taunt her about her black husband, and to give her advice similar to that Jimmie himself had received from the Nevilles:

> 'It's yore child, Mrs Blacksmith. But a white baby oughtn't let be grow up with tribal blacks.'

> 'It's yer chance!' Mrs Newby whispered. 'Yer'll only lose that child of yores if yer stay with the blacks.' (Ch.7)

For Gilda the moral torment is exacerbated by her suspicion that one of the Newby sons has bedded Miss Graf, and the knowledge that Mr Newby, in an obscene revelation of his unspoken fear of the Aborigines, had once exposed himself to her:

> Gilda always avoided him if she could, but he rolled up to her on his horse, vaulted out of the saddle and exposed his patriarchal genitals, slug-white and sitting in his hand for her information.
> 'When yer find a bigger'n than that on a nigger, Mrs Blacksmith, let me know.' (Ch.7)

The taunting of the Newby women, especially their unquestioning moral authority, arouses in Gilda painful memories of her orphanage childhood, and she is reduced to a roar of despair: 'She could not understand why she had no standing in the moral market-place' (Ch.7).

With the birth of her white child it is made clear to Jimmie that, for all the disdain with which Gilda has until then been treated, the white settlers are allied with her, and against him. Race outranks social class, and in the moral market-place Gilda's status after the birth is enhanced by an attitude whose crude philosophy had been expressed to Jimmie by Mr Newby himself, his words again echoing those of Rev. Neville on the desirable dilution of black blood: 'it doesn't matter how many times yer descendants bed down, they'll never get anything that don't have the tarbrush in it. And it'll spoil 'em, that little bit of somethink else' (Ch.6). Keneally's comment at this point – that such an attitude, while perhaps meant well in its way, 'implied fatal blindness in Jimmie's sense of what society allowed' (Ch.6) – foreshadows the mutually destructive entanglement of Newby's and Jimmie's fates.

A key concept in this novel is that of an individual's myths being 'overwhelmed' by what Keneally terms 'the realities of history': in Jimmie's case the determination even of the date of his execution by the minutiae of public policy is emblematic of such a process. Australia the nation did 'become a fact' in January 1901, and Keneally moves Jimmie's execution date from January to April in order to strengthen his point. 'History' in this sense is the received creation of those national fictions against which Jimmie fights but which, through his desperate acts of violence (not to mention his satisfaction at being reported in the press), he ironically ends by serving. The only identity he recognizes is that defined by white society.

There is also a strong sense, however, in which Keneally's book seeks to reassess official history against an alternative personal, tribal and racial history represented by the Aboriginal characters in the novel. As a half breed, Jimmie seems ideally placed to personify the dilemmas to which such a reassessment must inevitably lead, for the underlying fable of such a history ('the present merely rendered fabulous') is 'the contradiction between the avowed ideals of Australian nationhood and the actual values manifested in the treatment of the Aboriginals'. In this sense the book can be seen as an example of 'the creative writer responding and contributing to new appraisals of the values our society has inherited', a role that Keneally would undoubtedly accept with pleasure.

Some informed historical reaction to the book has, on the contrary, proved less than enthusiastic. Professor Henry Reynolds, an Australian scholar who has extensively researched settler relations with the Aborigines during the nineteenth century, and their legacy in Australian consciousness, feels that in his attribution of certain acts and responses to Jimmie's 'tribal instincts', 'Keneally confuses culture and biology, even if he is departing from the sources for aesthetic purposes'. Reynolds feels that the novel is 'very much a book of its time . . . written, published, read and reviewed in that period between 1969 and 1972 when white liberal opinion rediscovered the Aborigine – in the past and present, in history and in politics'. His conclusion is that at best the book 'captured an important aspect of the national mood at the time', but that at worst (like many Government policies at the time it was published) 'though superficially well meaning' it was 'paternalistic in execution, and burdened with an unconscious legacy of an ancestral racism'.[3] Keneally's claim to have written a book which tells Jimmie's story from the inside seems extraordinarily bold – foolhardy, even – but such claimed imaginative identification is neither more nor less extraordinary than that we encounter in his other books. In many respects it is less so, save the absolutely central questions of 'Australianness' and race themselves. These are questions on which Keneally's own opinion of his achievement has not been readily accepted: the contemporary Aboriginal writer Mudrooroo Narogin comments that in Keneally's book 'Aboriginal society is pictured as completely decayed. For the writer of Aboriginality this is not so.'[4] With the growth of Aboriginal, or 'Koori', fiction and criticism it will be interesting to see how Keneally's now-historical (1982) claim is regarded by a new generation of Australians.

3. Henry Reynolds, 'Jimmy Governor and Jimmie Blacksmith', *Australian Literary Studies*, 9/1, May 1979, pp.14–25. Reference on p.25. For a fuller study of Aboriginal/Settler culture contacts see Reynolds's *The Other Side of the Frontier: Aboriginal Resistance to the White Invasion of Australia*. A valuable lecture on this topic, 'The Breaking of the Great Australian Silence: Aborigines in Australian Historiography 1955–1983', first delivered by Professor Reynolds in London in 1948, is reprinted in Peter Quartermaine's, *Diversity Itself: Essays in Australian Arts and Cultures* (University of Exeter Press, 1968), pp.39–50.
4. Mudrooroo Narogin [the tribal name now used by Colin Johnson], *Writing from the Fringe: A Study of Modern Aboriginal Literature* (Hyland House, Melbourne, 1990), p.116.

4

'Civil' war: *Confederates*

History is a building whose goddam mortar is the blood of the young.
(*Confederates*)

The corollary of his belief in the vital historical importance of battle is Keneally's examination of how, through war, nations reckon that they kill themselves into history; bloodily enstate themselves in the record of human affairs. The author is particularly concerned with the ambivalent allegiance of Australians to such a proposition.
(Peter Pierce, 'The Sites of War in the Fiction of Thomas Keneally', 1986)

Internal conflict, especially that in which discord between warring elements of a single individual or institution is emblematic of a spiritual tension, is a wellspring of Keneally's writings: 'For Keneally, war has a central, if multi-faceted place in his apprehension of the destiny of individuals and nations, and of how these intersect'; a crucial aspect of such intersection is that 'In sex, in war, people fall apart. Their individuality is jeopardised.'[1] In this respect, the material for *Confederates* (1979) is ideally suited to his talents. The terrain of the American Civil War (1861–1865), duly featured on a map at the start of the volume, defines the geographical movement of events, but of equal interest for Keneally are the conflicting loyalties within

---

1. Peter Pierce, 'The Sites of War in the Fiction of Thomas Keneally', *Australian Literary Studies* (Brisbane), 12/4 October 1986, pp.442–452; reference on pp.443–448. An interview with Thomas Keneally by Laurie Hergenhan follows this article, pp.453–457.

the heart of those who fight (including those who fight on the same side nationally, but on opposite sides in personal terms). Generals and humble soldiers are equal in these conflicts, and victory and loss not easily apportioned. The book takes us from the second year of the war through to the Battle of Antietam Creek the following year, after which our guide and participant Usaph Bumpass, from Virginia, returns home; a brief final chapter narrates the fates of the main characters from this point to their deaths.

It is typical of Keneally's preoccupation with suffering, and with how human beings transcend it, that his novel focuses on the hopes and aspirations of the losing side in the Civil War; the well-informed historical perspective of author and reader lends a special poignancy to the conflicts and manoeuvres – military and emotional alike – which form the essence of the book. The bones of the novel trace various specific military and political events during the year 1862, but the reader's interest is always directed to occurrences at once more trivial and more significant. The Prologue opens with Mrs Bumpass having the unexpected pleasure of her soldier husband for an hour or so ('This happened way over in the great Valley of Virginia on a night of bitter frost'). The sexual pleasure they take in each other is, on the second page, already placed by Keneally in a context which both directly involves the national military conflict and invokes perspectives of divine judgement: 'The war she saw as a case of God making her pay for the sweetness and redemption that came to her in Usaph's presence – as simple as that. There wasn't anything in her life history to put that idea in her head either . . .' The opening of Book One balances this humble domestic episode by allowing the reader to glimpse none other than General 'Stonewall' Jackson as he awakes one morning:

> Four months later, on a morning in early July 1862, the young General Tom Jackson woke in a dusty bedroom in a rundown plantation house in Henrico County, Virginia. The house belonged to a Mr Thomas and was pretty typical of the sort of house slaveholders of middling wealth kept here in the Virginian lowlands. (1.Ch.1)

In scene-setting passages such as this Keneally grants the reader a sense of privileged access, as though to an intimate acquaintance of long standing. Phrases such as 'the young General Tom Jackson', together with the juxtaposition of the deliberately ordinary ('a dusty bedroom . . . a rundown plantation house') and the impressively specific ('Henrico County, Virginia') evoke the easy communication of knowledge which greatly exceeds the space/time available within the confines of the text. Keneally even employs lack of specificity to reinforce authorial control; the house is placed as 'pretty typical', so deflecting any excessive demands for detail on the part of the reader. That by the end of this first paragraph we are, as readers, already 'here' in the Virginian lowlands indicates the skill with which Keneally moves. At the end of the four-page opening chapter young Captain Pendleton races on horseback out of the front gate with General Jackson, and his thoughts seem precisely those that Keneally himself also intends to have established in the mind of the reader: 'This is what it is like to live . . . with a man who sees his job as being to whip history into shape.'

Just as important (to the soldiers) and engrossing (to the reader) as knowing what it is like to serve with such a man is knowing what it is like to die with him. When Jackson and Captain Pendleton arrive at the nearby wood from which Union troops can be observed, the text counterpoints its strong sense of place and time with images of foreboding. This is heightened when Jackson observes the Union troops through binoculars:

> even with the naked eye you could see the Federal camp on the James. Tents and waggons floated in a haze that still clung to the flats round Harrison's Landing. But with the binoculars you could see more. . . . Jackson could read their doubts as he gazed at them through the lenses.

The illusion of intimacy derived from the magnified observation of others often has its sinister side, most explicitly when done through a gunsight: 'a Yankee with a telescopic Whitworth rifle could study the distant man he was about to strike, the way you'd study the daguerrotype of your wife or brother' (1.Ch.3). To 'see more' is also to threaten. Keneally deliberately enhances this sense of control in claiming that General Jackson 'could read their doubts' as he watches them, a claim patently untrue; what *is* true is that Jackson's interpretation of the scene gains credibility with the reader through the magnified vision which it accompanies. Yet the claim that with binoculars one can 'see more' is doubtful; binoculars both magnify and exclude. The 'more' that they yield here is in the mind of Jackson (and Keneally), not in any better explanation of what the reader may 'see': as for the soldiers, they study those they will kill.

Confederates is a book of many and violent deaths, and of grue-somely extended battlefield horror of all kinds. Usaph's stomach (to his own disgust) signals its appetite as dead Union soldiers roast slowly in the burning grass of a railway embankment one fine summer's day

(3.Ch.9). His near despair at this inability to react appropriately as a complete human being (appetite pulling one way, morality another) signals a dilemma which informs much of the action in other spheres as well. The challenges of sudden death are highlighted early in the book, through the conversation between General Jackson and Captain Pemberton (Sandie):

> 'Tell me, Sandie,' said the General, holding a fat berry between forefinger and thumb, 'if you knew you were going to be shot and had a choice . . .'
>
> It was an eternal question of discussion. Generals and privates thought about it. With some the consideration became morbid. Others suspected that if they talked about the wound they wanted least it would stay away from them through some sort of sympathetic magic.
>
> Sandie thought and said: 'I just don't want one of those silly wounds, General. You know, the kind that shouldn't kill a man, but you bleed to death.'
>
> This wasn't quite the truth. Such deaths made him angry, but the deaths he really feared were wounds from artillery, and especially to be dismembered. (1.Ch.2)

Keneally cannot resist a punning reference to this 'eternal question', and *Confederates* provides generous descriptions of deaths mentioned and unmentioned by Sandie: in which a horse struggles 'up on its front legs out of a swamp of meat and cartilage' (2.Ch.7); a soldier is amazed to see a companion 'sit with his insides in his lap and ask for water' (2.Ch.10) and, after the din of battle, orderlies are to be seen stoking their gruesome fires 'with a human leg or arm' (2.Ch.11). The importance of graphic visual detail is emphasised by the soldier who had 'his right eye hanging by a sort of wormy stalk out on his cheek, where it was stuck in a sort of paste of blood' (2.Ch.12); the calculated imprecision of this description only sharpens the horror.

These passages allow the reader a chilling gaze at what the Irish poet W.B. Yeats termed 'the fury and the mire of human veins', the more so because Keneally stresses not only the chaos of the often ill-planned military/political process in which all the characters we follow are involved, but also the individually random nature of their deaths. For us, they live as individuals, but once dead they are mere statistics in what the United States forces in Vietnam would hideously term a 'body count'.

Keneally employs several narrative devices which emphasise both the pastness of the conflict we follow, and its unrelenting present for those involved. Early in the text Danny Blalock reads aloud an account of the projected course of the war from the American publication *De*

Bow's Review. The journal argues that only a spectacular coup by the
South would bring the British into the war, for example if they were 'to
capture Harrisburg, Pennsylvania, and descend on Baltimore from the
north by way of the Northern Central railroad (See Map) and then
on Washington itself!' (1.Ch.3). In this passage, Keneally's reader
(like that of *De Bow's*) is knowingly referred to the 'Map' (at the
front of *Confederates*), but Keneally complicates matters further by
having Danny himself meditate on the disparity between journalistic
theories and the reality of war:

> Danny thought it was easy for an editorialist to say '(See Map)'.
> These editorial writers didn't have to do any of the walking or
> wear through six pairs of boots as he had on Virginia's roads.
> (1.Ch.3)

In the same vein, Blalock is later described as arguing with another
soldier 'gallantly, just like something out of a novel' (1.Ch.4). Com-
bined with the devices discussed earlier, such sleight of hand by
Keneally seeks to convince the reader that the text is both more
and less than history: more, because (like the view we share with
Jackson through the lenses of the binoculars) it allows us to 'see
more'; less, since both its shape and its focus deliberately follow the
peculiarities of each individual character. It is precisely the myriad
differences between the human souls caught up in this conflict of
principles and politicians that hold Keneally's gaze, and is intended
to hold the reader's.

The chief way *Confederates* seeks to draw us into its world is
through the single narrative thread of soldier Usaph Bumpass, with
whom the Prologue had opened. We learn more of Usaph than of
any other figure in the novel, various generals and President Lincoln
included, and the well-founded suspicion and jealousy he has of Cate,
the itinerant portrait painter, brings onto the very field of battle those
domestic passions which would otherwise be entirely separate from the
military scene. Usaph does not pretend to understand the contradictions of a war that places Americans against each other, so that he can
stand picket with a Yankee on either side: 'That's what conscription
had done, put a Northerner on one flank and one of those Union-loving
boys from the western counties on the other' (2.Ch.2). He muses on
how the politicians would 'laugh over their goddam brandy' if they
knew, but his deeper thoughts are, as always, elsewhere:

> The deep tumour, the question that wouldn't cease its throb, was still
> whether Ephie had lain with his dead Uncle, that dead boozy man who

had engineered Ephie and him together, and now whether Cate had dazzled and possessed her. (2.Ch.2)

This dimension of Usaph's role in the book is complemented by that of the English journalist, the Honourable Horace Searcy, who personifies that privileged detachment earlier bemoaned by Danny Blalock. Where Usaph laments and fears his absence from his beloved Ephie, for Searcy this war is but one of series he has covered from an imperial perspective (albeit the one in which he also falls disastrously in love): 'His first war was the Crimean, then the war in Italy in '59, and finally the most vulgar of all wars, the conflict between all those former British colonies in North America' (1.Ch.9).

The perennial and intractable nature of military conflict, and especially the ambitions and disappointments it evokes, enables it to function as a metaphor for the greater struggle that is life itself. When the movement northward begins, it does so not 'because Tom Jackson, Kyd Douglas, Ephie Bumpass, Danny Blalock and *De Bow's Review* believed it should' (2.Ch.1), but because General Johnny Pope moves South. As Jackson, 'full of a quiet ecstasy', packs for the move he comments to Kyd: 'Battle is a Heraclitean thing. . . . Everything changes in war and if you don't believe so you lose' (2.Ch.1). It is through Usaph that the reader experiences the changes wrought by war, though not in the Heraclitean terms posed by Jackson:

> Usaph had first gone into what people liked to call a 'pitcher' or 'organised' battle on an afternoon in April near the village of Kernstown. From it alone he knew [battle to be] a mysterious event that could take you in any direction. (2.Ch.2)

In this first battle at Kernstown (which we learn of in retrospect, before following Usaph into battle a chapter later) Usaph was 'fighting for his own meadows and for the graves of his father and mother'; what he learns, however, is that 'there wasn't always much difference between the standfast and the man who ran', even though 'presidents and colonels and preachers tried to tell you otherwise' (2.Ch.2). In this respect he surprises himself with the dreadful ordinariness of battle, but before the reader witnesses a battle, blow for blow, Keneally makes his ordinariness very specific through a meeting between two friends of Usaph and two soldiers from the North. The four meet by chance in a wood, and agree to barter rather than fight:

> There ain't no sense fighting no equal-odds battle. Even if Henry and I shot you dead with our nice repeaters, what would it mean to anyone

but us? So Henry and I are wondering if you two boys're inclined to
trade and fraternise a little. Henry here now is busting for a scrap of
plug tobacco. You got any plug, Reb?
  'You got any coffee, Billy?' (2.Ch.2)

Such is the stuff of which enemies are made, and systems which
pit mankind against itself in spite of all natural instincts, or (on a
more sinister reading of human nature) provide free expression for
mankind's unchanging cruelties, never fail to absorb Keneally. Death
in battle for one's cause, martyrdom at the stake in the town square
for one's religion, is a moment in which, as T.S. Eliot expresses it in
Four Quartets, 'the timeless intersects with time.'
  The unpredictability of the battle we witness is heightened by the
'gimcrack factories of the South' which provide ammunition for the
artillery; Private Orville Puckett knows that each shell his gun crew
loads 'might, in twenty seconds' time, blow up anywhere between
the mouth of his cannon and the distant enemy' (2.Ch.7). Nor does
he harbour illusions about the details of death by artillery fire, noble
though death might once have been in another time, another place:

> Orville remembered a time in Lexington when they'd spent too long
> in a beer parlour and Maskill weeping in front of everybody about the
> death of Shelley. . . . When did that happen? Forty years past? Well,
> the world had lost all its innocence since then, and no Northern boy
> who was struck by Maskill's fire, or by his own, by Orville Puckett's,
> made any sort of decent corpse. (2.Ch.7)

Keneally's chronological placing of the battle through reference to
Shelley's death, and the poet's cremation 'right there on the sand
in the pink dawn by Lord Byron and other great men' (in 1822),
sharpens our interest in a conflict which will strip killing and death
of all dignity, all ceremony. Orville is only too aware that if the shot
from his No. 3 gun finds its target, then 'His own mother would swear
that that steaming meat there in the meadow was no flesh of hers'. The
Shelley reference also establishes the claim of Keneally's own text to
do for the likes of Orville Puckett and his friends what official literary
history has long since done for the English poet; to celebrate their lives
and deaths through the written word. This is also one of the mysterious
changes wrought by battle, appallingly down-to-earth as the business
of killing is:

> 'Well, the other rules is horse-sense. Single out an individual adversary
> for your fire, some man you've never met but you were destined to

make inroads in his life. Pick off the enemy's officers, particularly the ones like me who are mounted. . . . If you get their horses, they can't get the cannon away when we advance. . . . (2.Ch.8)

An irony of battle is that although bare practicality is the essence of killing, soldiers only respond to a crisis insofar as they lose that very rationality to which such tactical advice is addressed:

Jackson knew that men enraged like beasts were a gift to a general. Yet men in a Christian state were never meant to be enraged like beasts. Out of tensions and contradictions like this came the Lord's great day of justification and judgement. (2.Ch.8)

One aspect of the American Civil War which features only marginally in *Confederates* is the 'peculiar institution' of slavery. Book One had opened in a 'pretty typical' plantation house of 'middling wealth', and in events both on and off the battlefield Keneally chooses to stress the domesticity of slave society (at least from the whites' point of view) rather than seeking horrors. The greater military conflicts subsume those of slavery, and especially so for Decatur Cate, a Northerner who is conscripted into the Republican army. During battle he lies for a time beside the corpse of a young 'enemy' second lieutenant:

What did it really matter to a boy from Michigan if South Carolina or Virginia wished to manage itself? What did it matter to him if there were slaves in the South? . . . Cate felt sure that this dead boy was, in the springtime he got this coat of his measured and cut, just about like most other Northerners. If they wanted slaves freed, it was for religious and moral reasons, as much because it debased Southern whites as for the fact it enslaved blacks. Or had there been in fact a scalding desire for the equality of blacks in this particular boy's chest? Well, it was lulled now. (2.Ch.10)

Cate's own reaction to such meditations is to curse 'the eyes and livers and genitals of those men who'd pushed the issue to the extent that boys from Michigan came down to the farms of Virginia to be killed among the corn'. This bitter harvest feeds the reputations of politicians and the careers of generals rather than the modest aspirations of ordinary people, but it is the generals and politicians who control it: 'It's a war to be deplored, but it's in progress' (2.Ch.10).

Cate's previous experience of slavery had been in the household of Ephie Bumpass, and on the day he arrived Keneally tells us that it was 'operating in a way that would have delighted those who wanted to argue that slavery was a humane and Christian institution', and suggests some practical reasons for the prevailing rural harmony of butter-churning and singing that pervades the verandahs:

> slavery only worked for the rich. . . . The trap was that many people could only manage to have that true Virginian high-handedness with slaves if they owned a few hundred of them. If you owned a few, those few tended to become members of the family. You couldn't rightly sell them even in bad times, because when you tried they wailed and begged you not to and it was like selling a brother. You fretted through their layings-in and their births, through their illnesses and their long dotage. And some of them sure had a long, long dotage! (2.Ch.14)

It is very much into the spirit of such a unified household, where each person carries out an allotted task, that Decatur Cate enters as a travelling portrait painter – and seducer of Ephie. Just as war is a great leveller of rank and race, so the bonds of family, and of individual passion will prove the arbiters of Cate's destiny (one aspect of which will be his own forced conscription into the same regiment as the man whose wife he has seduced): 'Neither Decatur Cate approaching the house, not Aunt Sarrie nor Ephie inside it, were thinking of the ironies of the peculiar institution [slavery] that leafy spring morning when Decatur Cate left his surrey at the gate . . .' (2.Ch.14).

In the romantic attachment Cate forms with Ephie, as much as in the impossible situation in which he later finds himself as an unwilling soldier on the wrong side, Keneally's interest lies in exploring how individual lives are entangled in a history not of their making, rather than in analysing the moral issues which feed the conflict. In this respect, as *Jimmie Blacksmith* had suggested, the aims and motives of a murderer and a hangman may come uncomfortably close. For hero and victim alike the pressures derive from acute awareness of 'the big forces of history working away, and if you let them big wheels grind, and sat small and easy on their rim, you might escape being mashed down to pap by them' (2.Ch.15). Such are Cate's thoughts, but they no longer convince after direct experience of battle, and ever since that chastening experience he had been 'pale as a sick aunt and looked like he couldn't crawl out of the way of one of them great wheels if they was to come rolling across the encampment fields right now'.

The extent to which individuals see themselves as shaping, or being shaped by, history finds natural expression in a novel centred on civil war and the defining of national destiny. At its most effective this sense of oppressive historical tradition on the one hand, and of seemingly limitless possibilities on the other, is expressed through sharp images of wonderfully immediate and accessible description. 'In the glare of a big clearing' Usaph and others of the Shenandoah Volunteers come upon prisoners digging a mass grave for themselves. Usaph is shocked by the disciplined brutality of the process – 'How did they choose them' – but the overwhelming sense of mortality at this crucial moment is displaced to the land, to the very element from which they are literally shaping their own imminent destiny. Keneally's sharp sense of detailed unimportance endows the moment with menace while placing the events we are about to witness in that wider context where some would claim brutality can be researched, structured and understood as 'history':

> The afternoon was hot, full of a blur of flies and the screaming of katydids. The vast meadow where they stood was like a sort of history of America itself. It sat amongst ancient forests. It had been cleared maybe about 1760 by some Scot, some Irishman, some sharp Yorkshireman. It had borne more crops than a sow has litters for a century or more, but now its owner did not much esteem it, or was happy to let it rest, for blackberries grew in clumps there, the grass was high, and the forest that had preceded the farmers was growing back at the edges. America was not however easily cancelled. (2.Ch.18)

Keneally is always drawn to images which can be seen as symbolising wider issues, a natural enough instinct for a novelist. Searcy is granted exactly such authorial tendencies as he travels in a Southern steamboat on the Mississippi:

> a visit to the engine room, where blacks naked to the clout thrust whole pine beams into the mouth of the boilers, convinced you the whole light, over-driven structure would explode any second. In contrast, life on the upper decks was pretty gracious by Southern standards. The whole ship . . . seemed to Searcy like a great floating symbol of the South itself. (2.Ch.26)

In Keneally's writing life remains an unresolved, and unresolvable, muddle of virtue and sin, heroism and turpitude. The literal shambles that is war, 'putting dead into three pits – one for the Union, one for the Confederacy, and one for corpses that carried no signs other than those of their humanity' (3.Ch.11), is also an aspect of the struggle in which humanity is perpetually engaged: to reconcile an intractable moral environment with its sense of righteousness. In such a world even a clergyman who dies on the field of battle, as does The Reverend

Dignam, departs in an uncertainty occasioned by his infidelity to his wife on two occasions with 'Mrs Alison Kane, wife of the presiding elder of the county':

> The memory of her face sat in his mind now like a single live and well creature in a doomed house. And he was free to cling onto it all the way down that tunnel that opened beneath him and drank him down. And even as he fell he accused himself. For soldiering had been vanity and the war had been a gift to him, getting him away from Mrs Dignam, a fine girl he failed to love through no fault of hers, and away from the sharp thoughts of Mrs Alison Kane. (3.Ch.3)

Such are our privileged insights into Dignam's thoughts at the moment of death – that moment to which Keneally returns again and again, seeking with ever more imaginative imagery to apprehend in advance the secrets it might hold. Dignam's friend and companion, Colonel Lafcadio Wheat, reads events rather differently in the passage which follows immediately: 'from the feel of the preacher's limbs, he could tell already that one of the best and most sensible of men had perished in an instant of time'. Keneally is fascinated not so much by the contrast between the two views – private guilt and public virtue – as by their simultaneous truth, just as in the same battle Usaph comes to share General Jackson's realisation that there can be no true reconciliation, but only a juxtaposition, of the teachings of the Bible and the demands of warfare:

> He guessed that if he touched a scripture at a time like this he'd lose his call on those war-hungry devils that got into him at times like these. And without those devils, he couldn't face fire.
>
> Bumpass, the war animal, fired four rounds before the Union colonels got over their craziness and stopped despatching boys over that small rise. (2.Ch.3)

The impossibility, for the author as well as the participant, of reconciling such disparate demands and motivations will later animate the story of Oskar Schindler, Nazi-consorting black market racketeer and saviour of Jews. It seems that the author's own response to these contradictory stimuli is recourse to the pleasure of storytelling itself, contradictions and all. Characters in Keneally's books who are confronted by equally fragmenting demands certainly display awareness on occasions of the recompenses of narrative. Here Lafcadio Wheat nears the end of a tale:

Both Gus and Usaph were in now, and Usaph had forgotten the question of Ephie. For this was a tale of such villainy. And Wheat thought, even in the enthusiasm of his story-telling, 'I'm binding you two boys to me by the magic of my narrative.' (3.Ch.6)

The role of Searcy, a professional observer of wars (and spy) and an Englishman to boot, is illuminating here for his fate is to become part of the conflict he thought only to report. Mrs Dora Whipple, the lady spy with whom he falls in love, warns him early of the extent to which they both 'labour under the circumstances of this war' (2.Ch.2), and later Searcy himself comes to understand that there is never any escape from war:

The sense that he was fatally locked to this foreign war frightened him. He had always been an observer before, it was a role that suited his unattached soul. He's never felt a particular war would get him. He felt it now . . . this war wouldn't let him off free as all the others had. (3.Ch.14)

Nothing better captures the manner in which Searcy slips from the role of observer to that of endangered participant than the scene in which he composes his description of the Battle of Antietam Creek, a description steeped in classical-historical consciousness, unawares that he himself is about to be arrested for his undercover activities:

He tried to write in an objective style, as if he had no stake in the outcome of whatever happened here in these low ridges, in these country lanes among the low hills.

Inwardly, of course, he knew that these pleasant hills behind a stream called Antietam Creek had been chosen by whatever forces act in these matters, as the venue for one of this earth's crucial fights – just as the same forces, half a century before, had picked out the environs of a Belgian village named Waterloo. . . . (3.Ch.2)

Searcy sees himself as an educated man (he is upset as much by the vulgarity of Americans on both sides of the conflict as by any horrors of war) and can articulate the recurrent patterns of historical process with some elegance. Others embroiled in the conflict are less privileged, less fluent, but their perceptions grope towards that patterning which Searcy takes for granted. Cate replies to a question from Bumpass as to why he stays in the war as follows:

'I stay, Bumpass,' said Cate, and Usaph couldn't make out whether he was joking or bitter, 'because I got this view of history. I see that you and me, Bumpass, in all our present discomfort, are dead in the heart of history, like currants in a cake.' (4.Ch.1)

Cate, too, has his sense of historical precedent and asks Bumpass whether he has ever heard of Hannibal and 'an old battle called Cannae' before going on to define his own sense of historical process, and his own part in it. It is a definition which, bringing together as it does youth and death, the momentary and the timeless, might be seen as a fitting indication of Keneally's own attitude to history and its story:

> History is a river, Bumpass, in which you and I are the fish. Have you ever caught a river perch, Bumpass, and when he lay panting wondered if he'd had a happy morning before you hauled him ashore? Did you wonder what his passions were . . . what the poor son of a bitch had had for breakfast? Neither does God or history enquire such things of us, Bumpass. Yet without us, God and history would not be a river. That's the puzzle, Bumpass, that keeps us here. (4.Ch.1)

Usaph's furious reaction to Cate's detached and philosophical attitude to contemporary events is expressed in imagery reminiscent of the 'ringside seat to history' phrase from *Jimmie Blacksmith*: 'You tell me, Cate, you're travelling around with us jest to see the circus? Goddamit, Cate, you ain't even decent' (4.Ch.1). But Usaph's role throughout the novel is that of a genuine innocent whose awareness of larger issues is always severely limited by his – all too human – preoccupation with more immediate emotions, especially his overwhelming love for his wife, Ephie. It is to Ephie that Cate's thoughts also turn in the heat of battle, when it seems that 'God and history are going to swallow' him:

> Oh yes, Cate decided with the workaday despair of the damned, we're going to die right together here. Sublime Ephie can be some sort of double widow and go uncomforted. And so he just stood there and gave himself up to the darkest forces of history.' (4.Ch.6)

After events, Searcy reads the story of the final battle and its outcome with very different feelings, concerned (much as the historian is) with concepts of broad purpose and morality, rather than with fear of dying. His focus is on the river, not the fish:

> Why, knowing everything, hadn't McClellan managed to trap the beast, the Secession itself, the Serpent of Slavery between Antietam Creek and the big river that morning and so ended it all? It was a

question he would bore people with for some years to come. It was
the old question of how such incompetence could go hand in hand
with a good cause. (4.Ch.8)

In the scheme of things as depicted by Keneally, consciousness of a
'good cause' parallels the overall shaping of history; 'incompetence'
is history as made and seen by fallible individuals. As Keneally himself
makes very clear in the passages quoted above, 'history' is of course
always made by individuals; yet all of us as individuals seek shape
and pattern in any sequence of events. Only too conscious of our
insignificance as fishes, we seek always to discern the shape of the
river: the longing is as definitive of what it means to be human as the
sense of disappointment, even disillusion, which may well follow.

True to such a discomforting view of history, *Confederates* ends not
with wise meditations on the progress, or otherwise, represented by the
Civil War, but with a very downbeat series of anecdotal conclusions
to the various personal stories whose interweavings have constituted
the bulk of war as we – as reader – have seen it. The complete
disjunction in personal experience between the decisions of generals
and politicians and the daily lives of simple folk is graphically imaged
through the return of Usaph Bumpass to his own home, unrecognised
and unrecognisable:

> On the afternoon of September 14 that year, the black woman Bridie
> who belonged to Aunt Sarrie and knew nothing about the intentions
> Mr Abe Lincoln had for her, went out on the porch to fetch in a mat
> she'd been sunning out there. The valley was full of that blue autumn
> shadowiness, but she could see clear enough a ragged man standing
> still at the gate. The man wore his wrist in a foul linen sling and
> stood there wavering a little on his legs but with his feet fixed in
> place. (4.Ch.11)

The ending of the book is very much a tidying up of loose ends,
of satisfying the quite justifiable curiosity – but little more – that the
reader will have as to what happened to characters who separately
are of modest interest only. For them, as for the Reverend Dignam,
the war we have followed with them has been in unsuspected ways 'a
gift', decidedly mixed in its blessings but raising them from the plain
of ordinary life to the high ground of suffering and, sometimes, vision
(or nightmare).

The closing words of the novel are the last words of General
Stonewall Jackson, just before he died 'on the afternoon of May
10', 1863, in the Chandler's house in Chancellorsville: 'Let us cross

over the river and rest under the shade of the trees.' In their colloquial simplicity and accessibility, as much as in their Biblical foreshadowing (conscious or not) of approaching death, these words come as close as may be to encapsulating the qualities which the book has explored. In these terms it is a fitting ending to a grand theme. The reader may nevertheless feel uneasy at the extent to which, here as elsewhere in the book:

> the part is persistently promoted to the whole. Fragmented individual experience is willed to become a grand matter more of soul than of body, more of mankind's destiny than one man's . . . Keneally wishes the fragments of the great war which he describes to stand – really without qualification – as a true account of the whole conflict.[2]

This issue, and especially the historical and moral burden carried by one individual, is central to the next novel discussed, *Schindler's Ark*.

2. Peter Pierce, 'Recent Fiction: Futurism and Other Projections', *Meanjin* (Melbourne), 39/2 July 1980, pp.260–269. Reference on p.264.

5

One man's war: *Schindler's Ark*

We are all predisposed to praise books by concentration camp survivors; and indeed no record of that most terrible of experiences can be without value. Under the circumstances, it usually seems tactless to raise questions of literary merit. . . . Yet the sad fact is that the quality of the writing *does* count, however harrowing the subject, and that much of [Holocaust] literature . . . is effective only at the level of poignant documentary. To have been a witness, and a survivor, and a born writer was a rare combination.
(John Gross, quoted in the Introduction to the Penguin edition of *If not Now, When?* by Primo Levi)

In time every event becomes an exertion of memory and is thus subject to invention. The further the facts, the more history petrifies into myth. Thus, as we grow older as a race, we grow aware that history is written, that it is a kind of literature without morality . . . that everything depends on whether we write this fiction through the memory of hero or victim.
(Derek Walcott, 'The Muse of History', 1974)

If the Holocaust had not occurred, to write about such events would be to make a kind of science fiction. Since the Holocaust really did occur, I suppose you could call it real science fiction which happened in the past; history's most astounding and compelling science fiction.
(Thomas Keneally, 1989)

The publication in 1982 of *Schindler's Ark* marked a high point – it may yet be seen as *the* high point – in Keneally's career. The book (and to call it a novel is to beg the question raised by the quotations above) won the prestigious Booker McConnell Prize (*Jimmie Blacksmith*, *Gossip from the Forest* and *Confederates* had all been shortlisted when published) and so convincingly established Keneally's reputation as an international writer. The book's subject also involved Keneally grappling, albeit tangentially, with the most terrible and prolonged 'event' of modern history; the carefully-planned programme of Hitler's Nazi Germany which (though never completed) killed some six million Jews, together with hundreds of thousands of other people. In tackling this fearful subject, and in a secular age such as ours it may be thought the greatest subject that modern history offers (equal in import to Milton's choice of 'paradise lost' for his epic poem), Keneally also makes a detailed consideration of his approach to fact and to fiction inevitable.

Whether, and if so exactly how, the undoubted impact of *Schindler's Ark* – including its impact on the 1982 Booker judges – depends upon any reader's instinctive sympathy for the victims of Hitler's 'final solution' is hard to say. Unquestionably, though, in the bizarre story of fine-living Oskar Schindler's determination to save Jews by employing them in his factory, ostensibly to produce material for the German war effort, Keneally found a series of events at once so extraordinary – even unbelievable – and so compelling that they were the perfect material for his particular fusion of history and personality. In a very special way this proves the accuracy of Peter Pierce's comment on Keneally's war writing.

> The handling of war in Keneally's fiction is in large measure a transposition of family romance, of domestic melodrama.
>   His portrayals of war and its consequences are claustrophobic rather than panoramic. Key scenes are more often indoors than on the field.[1]

A consideration of the book's effect on the reader can usefully begin at the very beginning, with the book's launch and subsequent presentation by its publishers. The background story of the book's emergence into print, including its differing prepublication advertisement as 'fiction', 'non-fiction novel' and, finally, 'fiction-with-an-Author's-Note', is well charted by Terry Downie in the 1989 *Textplus* edition, which includes an excellent selection of various contextual material, historical and critical. In the 1982 Sceptre paperback edition (published after the award of the Booker Prize) our very approach to the text is

1. Peter Pierce, *The Sites of War*, p.444.

undoubtedly conditioned by the accompanying critical assurances as much as by detailed factual apparatus (three maps and a Glossary of 'SS Ranks and Their Army Equivalents'). In similar vein, the dedication is 'To the memory of Oskar Schindler, and to Leopold Pfefferberg who by zeal and persistence *caused this book to be written*' (my emphasis), where Keneally seeks to displace any imaginative source for the book in favour of it being 'caused' by the 'zeal' of a Schindler survivor. Thirteen unreservedly approving comments by writers ranging from Graham Greene to Alan Sillitoe, and from journals ranging from the *Sunday Express* to the *New York Review of Books* praise the power, detail and beauty of the 'story' (a recurrent term) that Keneally tells, and the *New York Times Book Review* captures the general feeling in its comment that 'This remarkable book has the immediacy and the almost unbearable detail of a thousand witnesses who forgot nothing'. Keneally himself explains in the *Textplus* (TP) edition that the book was written at his New South Wales house near 'a beautiful little sun-drenched, sub-tropic beach, a long way in time, place and spirit from the terrible era with which the book is concerned' (TP p.iv). To claim the immediacy of first-hand witness and the status of undiminished memory for such a book, especially when it is awarded a major fiction prize, is an act of some daring.

Keneally contributes his own powerful dimension to the suggested acceptance of literary text as historical testimony by recounting in his two-page Author's Note ('signed' in facsimile 'Tom Keneally') how he chanced upon the 'cause' of the book in a Beverly Hills luggage shop:

> Beneath Pfefferberg's shelves of imported Italian leather goods, I first heard of Oskar Schindler, the German *bon vivant*, speculator, charmer, and sign of contradiction, and of his salvage of a cross-section of a condemned race during those years now known by the generic name, Holocaust.'

Life here matches art, or at least artistic preference, in the way that all artists and writers understandably sift and select incidents from the shapeless chaos that is daily life. And the author himself addresses directly the delicate balance of fact and fiction which informs the book throughout:

> To use the texture and devices of a novel to tell a true story is a course which has frequently been followed in modern writing. It is the one I have chosen to follow here; both because the craft of the novelist is the only craft to which I can lay claim, and because the novel's techniques

> seemed suited for a character of such ambiguity and magnitude as
> Oskar. I have attempted to avoid all fiction, though, since fiction would
> debase the record, and to distinguish between reality and the myths
> which are likely to attach themselves to a man of Oskar's stature.

Keneally here accepts the need to use imagination – 'texture and
devices', as he puts it – in fleshing out the bones of historical facts,
especially in scenes of dialogue in direct speech (hardly the form in
which most records tend to be kept). He is insistent, though, on his
concern to avoid all fabrication and to maintain the truth of what he
interestingly terms, at the end of a lengthy list of acknowledgements,
his 'project'. One explanation as to why he has felt this possible is
that Oskar's recorded achievements were so 'outrageous' that they
exceeded any fiction a novelist might dare. Keneally argues in his
Introduction to the *Textplus* edition that 'Oskar's story, though it
is true, has many of the qualities and excitements of fiction', but in
his Author's Note to the original edition explained that selection and
shaping were unavoidable:

> Sometimes it has been necessary to attempt to reconstruct conversations
> of which Oskar and others have left only the briefest record. But most
> exchanges and conversations, and all events, are based upon the detailed
> recollections of the *Schindlerjuden* (Schindler Jews), of Schindler him-
> self, and of other eyewitnesses to Oskar's acts of outrageous rescue.

The text proper, beginning with a nineteen-page section entitled
'PROLOGUE AUTUMN 1943', opens in a way which extends the
significance of such questions for the reader. Cinema-like, the author
swoops in on the character whose life and work we will follow
throughout the book: 'In Poland's deepest autumn, a tall young man
in an expensive overcoat, double-breasted dinner-jacket beneath it and
– in the lapel of the dinner jacket – a large ornamental gold-on-black
enamel swastika'. In a sentence reminiscent of the sudden opening
of *Bring Larks and Heroes* we are already drawn in by 'texture and
devices' more characteristic of fiction than history, but Keneally seeks
to preempt any unease the reader might feel:

> In observing this winter scene, we are on safe ground.
>
> . . .
>
> But it will not be possible to see the whole story under such easy
> character headings. For this is the story of the pragmatic triumph of
> good over evil, a triumph in eminently measurable, statistical, unsubtle
> terms. . . . Fatal human malice is the staple of narrators, original sin
> the mother-fluid of historians. But it is a risky enterprise to write of
> virtue. (Prologue)

Risky it may be, but in the context of earlier novels Keneally's attraction to Oskar's story is understandable, not only for its inextricable
linking of the personal and the historical but also since potentially
it exemplifies a Biblical scale of damnation and redemption in the
working out of its 'triumph of good over evil'. As Keneally comments
of a later incident, 'It is a scene, a speech worthy of one of those
events in the Old Testament when for the good of the tribe a woman
is offered to the invader', though he continues, characteristically
but hardly convincingly, to suggest other (and all too stereotypical)
historical and ethnic qualities: 'It is also a Central European scene,
with its gross, coruscating diamonds and its proposed transaction of
the flesh'. (Ch.33)

The specific, even eccentric, story of Oskar Schindler and his Jewish
workers is also, for Keneally, yet another illustration of humanity's
infinite capacity for contradiction and conflict. In bringing such qualities alive for the reader Keneally perforce treads a tricky path, where
a phrase such as 'Only he could have told us' (Prologue) asserts the
author's status as reliable narrator at the same time as it signals the
impossibility of complete reliability; the skill of the novelist must
in such instances – with the allowance of the reader – supplant
the testimony of the witness. In Chapter 5, for instance, Keneally
demonstrates how adept he is at achieving the delicate shift from
flagged reconstruction to the privileged viewpoint of dinner guest at
a party of Oskar and Nazi officials. The passage begins with the open
statement: 'Though it is not possible to say exactly what the members
of the party talked about that night, it is possible from what Oskar said
later of each of these men to make a plausible reconstruction'. So when
the passage continues with the sentence 'It would have been Gebauer
who made the toast . . .' the reader can accept it on these terms, as
a likely supposition. What should the reader make, though, of the
short paragraph which introduces the major topic of that evening's
talk: 'But after the toast had been drunk, the talk turned naturally to
the subject that bemused or obsessed all levels of the civil bureaucracy.
The Jews'? By a magical, if disturbing, sleight of hand Keneally so
contrives it that as (*then,* supposedly) 'the talk turned naturally' to the
subject of the Jews so, too (*now*), does our perspective 'turn naturally'
from that of a reader of history to that of a fellow guest at table. We
may accept the likelihood of such tabletalk; but we may question the
literary device by which we are lured into accepting it as 'witnessed'
history. Such scenes illustrate Keneally's belief that while 'people in
the grip of history are overcome with a sense of unreality', most people
engaged in historic events (he cites the *New York Times* journalists in

the Watergate affair) are *not* aware of making history: 'people just go on behaving like themselves in moments of high history'.[2]

If Keneally is anxious to evoke what he sees as the 'Central European' aspect of Oskar's story he is equally determined that his character's role should not be limited in time and place, and seeks to establish this not only through an immediacy with Oskar from the start but also through an attempt at cultural shorthand which stresses that outsider quality common to so many of Keneally's flawed heroes and heroines:

> There is no doubt that in their way the police chiefs and the commandant liked Oskar. There was, however, something odd about him. They might have been willing to write it off in part to his origins. He was Sudeten German, Arkansas to their Manhattan, Liverpool to their Cambridge. (Prologue)

But if Oskar is outside the social establishment, he is also (and needs to be for Keneally's fictional purposes) outside the very processes of history which under one aspect define his story. Nothing better suggests this timeless relevance of religious epic – and simultaneously emphasises its disjunction from the everyday world – than an early scene in which Oskar observes to Itzhak Stern that it must be hard to be a priest in these days 'when life does not have the value of a packet of cigarettes'. Stern's response expresses the truth will later be engraved on a ring cast from dental fillings donated by Oskar's grateful Jewish workers: 'He who saves a single life, saves the world entire' (Ch.2). It is Talmudic verse which in religious terms encapsulates the inviolable sanctity of the individual human life; it also, from the viewpoint of the novelist seeking to convey the meaning of the Holocaust within 400-odd pages, suggests the key to Keneally's imaginative representation of events. The story of Oskar and his ark (whether we see the latter as analogous to that of Noah or of the Jewish Covenant) is a story unique in its scale and daring, and able to stand as emblem for the inherent divinity and corruption of humanity itself.

In retrospect we can appreciate the unpredictable combination of individuality and wealth, history and race, that was to shape Oskar Schindler's life, and Keneally stresses this in telling how Leopold Pfefferberg, the very man from whom he was to hear Oskar's story

2. Michael Fabre, 'Thomas Keneally: an interview', *Caliban*: Annales de l'Universitaire de Toulouse-Le Mirail, 14, N.S., XIII (1975), pp.101–8. Reference on p.105.

in that Beverly Hills shop forty years later, almost shot Oskar in the autumn of 1939:

> If the magnetic drift to the event had drawn Pfefferberg to fire, the death, the flight, the reprisals would have been considered unexceptional and appropriate to the history of the month. . . . And back in Zwittau they would have said, 'Was it someone's husband?' (Ch.3)

Towards the close of the book Keneally quotes the insight of Oskar's widow that her husband's capacity for doing good might have gone forever unrealised had not particular political, social and economic circumstances made him a potential employer when they did:

> Perceptively, she remarked that Oskar had done nothing astounding before the war and had been unexceptional since. He was fortunate therefore that in that short fierce era between 1939 and 1945 he had met people who had summoned forth his deeper talents. (Epilogue)

Although not stated, the import of this perception is that each and every one of us has great potential for good (and, equally, for evil), though for most of us circumstances will never require (or allow) it to be realised; we remain, in the words of Gray's *Elegy*, 'mute, inglorious Miltons'. In this sense, too, it is suggested that Schindler stands for us all. In what sense, though, can Oskar Schindler stand for us all when the shaping elements of his story are so specific in time and place, and so extraordinary (as the author himself emphasises) that they are unlikely to be repeated?

One answer is that the scale of the Holocaust itself places it, and the period in which it took place, in a mythic dimension which allows us to read its events and personalities with an immediacy which spans the decades. The book is set, according to the Sceptre edition jacket blurb, in 'the shadow of Auschwitz'. The shadow is indeed there, but *Schindler's Ark* avoids the mass slaughter of the concentration camps for the equally shocking, and shocking precisely because more mundane, *minutiae* of daily life:

> author and reader alike become engrossed by the obscenity of the process whereby something as horrendous as the 'final solution' can be expressed in terms of supply and demand, train timetables, consignment notes.[3]

---

3. David English, *History and the Refuge of Art*, p.27.

The book does contain sequences in Auschwitz, to which a group of Schindler's women workers are transported, but only as part of the ongoing story of Oskar and 'his' Jews; the narrative focus is always upon the shifting relationships of protection and dependency. Eventually, inevitably it seems, Oskar succeeds in rescuing his Jews and the immediate horrors of the mass extermination camps are replaced by the more intimate and apparently controllable dangers of the 'factory family' whose fate the reader follows throughout. As Keneally himself put it:

> The book deals mainly with the period in which Schindler became protector, big brother, parent to his prisoners. But then, after the terrible times ended, roles shifted utterly and with an almost artistic neatness, Schindler became the child. (TP p.iv)

Such a focus has many reasons, and many advantages. The obvious reason is that Keneally's own interest was in the single life of Oskar Schindler, a life with 'shape to it' which was 'very appropriate for a novelist to write about it, even if it happens to be the truth' (TP p.iv). From the reader's point of view, the advantage of such a focus is that it avoids the greatest danger in our reaction today to events of overwhelming horror and suffering: indifference. In early 1991, some two weeks into the Gulf War, public complaints were voiced in Britain that the conflict was receiving excessive coverage on television, and that viewers were wearying of the unrelenting information provided by that same global communications technology that characterised the so-called 'smart weapons' with which the war was waged.

The problem is that much of our global information, 'The News', lacks exactly that shape – and therefore that meaning and relevance – which Keneally sees it as the business of the novelist to provide: 'Where is the knowledge we have lost in information?' lamented Eliot in 'The Rock'. Keneally's comment, in the epigraph to this chapter, that the Holocaust itself can perhaps be seen as science fiction set in the past is revealing here, bringing together as it does the imaginative possibilities of the future and the historical parable – as Keneally would see it – of the past. It is a powerful combination which, if accepted by the reader, grants the writer a formidable authority. Certainly it is one well suited to Keneally's own technique for the depiction of historical event which, as we have seen, strives always to convey the general through the specific, and to offer the reader 'a ringside seat to history'. Applied to Oskar's story the technique has special advantages, as even a sceptical commentator on the book grants:

> [the book] is a monumental and engrossing treatment of the Second
> World War because, thoroughly in accord with Keneally's minimalist
> smart-aleck view of historical cause and effect, most of the crea-
> tive energy is spent establishing that the shooting and battlefield
> manoeuvring has only a small place in the texture of the routine
> life of a country at war.[4]

The 'minimalist' view demands that such violence as the reader does
encounter shock more by its sudden and chance nature than in its
scope or duration: Commandant Amon's random shootings from
the 'domestic' comfort of his house verandah perfectly typify this.
The machinery and the paperwork required by the larger plans of
the extermination camps is also deliberately left to shock by its very
tediousness: 'Seen in peacetime, the gallows of Plaszow and Auchswitz
would intimidate not by their solemnity but by their ordinariness'
(Ch.24).

Keneally's documentary method places the reader always in the
position of survivor: the author creates the sensation of a ringside
seat to history, but of course we are never really in any danger of
being caught up in those events whose unfolding we follow with
interest − and, yes, enjoyment. Our survival is guaranteed by our
status as reader, even as we see the mesmerising randomness of death
under Amon Goeth's administration. Mundek Korn, a clerk at the
camp, witnesses a killing from his office, which is in the same wing
as Amon's:

> One morning Korn looked up from his desk and saw through the
> window, across Jerozolimska Street and by the SS barracks, a boy
> of twenty years or so, a Cracovian of his acquaintance, urinating
> against the base of one of the stacks of timber there. At the same
> time he saw white-shirted arms and two ham fists appear through
> the bathroom window. The right hand held a revolver. There were
> two quick shots, at least one of which entered the boy's head and
> drove him forward against the pile of cut wood. When Korn looked
> once more at the bathroom window, one white-shirted arm and free
> hand were engaged in closing the window. (Ch.26)

Keneally coldly observes that workers such as Korn faced 'not only a
daily risk of an unexpected bullet but, more certainly than that, assaults
on their sense of outrage'. In such a world Keneally's lasting fascination
with violence and with the unpredictable quirks of human nature

---

4. Ibid.

finds unlimited sanction; as readers we must also admit the unique satisfaction to be had from reading tales of death and destruction which do not directly involve us. In the context of this novel we might well be wary of admitting to such a motive, but the cover of the Sceptre edition, with the Jewish Star of David woven in barbed wire, leaves little doubt of what the purchaser is offered.

The teasing relationship between narrative fiction and the unfolding of contemporary history is raised obliquely by Keneally in a concentration camp scene:

> 'Don't kill yourself on the fence, Clara,' the woman urged her. 'If you do that, you'll never know what happened to you.' It has always been the most powerful of answers to give to the intending suicide. Kill yourself and you'll never find out how the plot ends. Clara did not have any vivid interest in the plot. But somehow the answer was adequate. She turned around. (Ch.33)

It is characteristic of Keneally to raise and then deflect the issue with the casual phrase, 'somehow the answer was adequate'. For both reader and author, though, the interchange briefly signals the complex interrelation of those very parallels between the narrative structures of fiction and those of historical events which first drew Keneally to Oskar Schindler's 'lifestory', a term whose colloquial usage can encompass the expectations of both real-life experience and of fiction.

For Oskar and the others, actors in the lifestory we follow, motive and meaning are often unclear; their point of view is more limited than that of reader or of author. Saved by the young brother of a girl he had once taught, Pfefferberg himself (the prime 'cause' of the book) 'had no leisure to thank the boy or to reflect on the mystery of why a child with a skinny neck will lie for you just even unto the death just because you once taught his sister how to use the vaulting horse' (Ch.13). Such 'mystery' in the overall story, the imponderable capacity of human nature for unlimited good and evil, is partly what draws Keneally to the tale. A very different mystery informs the complex system of bureaucracy necessary to execute and document the processes of the Holocaust. When Oskar saves a group of his workers from a train destined for the gas chambers, the final response of the German guard charged with the consignment grants us a glimpse into this world view:

> The officer had been frowning when Oskar first saw him, but now seemed calm as if he had discovered the theorem behind the situation. You think your thirteen little tinsmiths are important? We'll replace

them with another thirteen little tinsmiths and all your sentimentality for these will be defeated. 'It's the inconvenience to the list, that's all,' the officer explained in the end. (Ch.14)

This sense of there not being an adequate explanation for human actions (good or bad) is often characteristic of life as we live it; the value of religion in such a world is precisely that it offers a peace which passeth all understanding. Keneally instances exactly this sense of mystery, of incompleteness, as an attractive quality (for him as author) of Oskar's lifestory:

> The book has been criticised by some for not giving a full accounting of Schindler's motives. I don't think such a full accounting is possible in Schindler's case. *He wasn't the sort of man who spent a lot of time asking himself about his reasons for doing things* . . . if you add up every possible element of motivation, then you are still left with a quotient of mystery. (TP p.vi, my emphasis)

More generally, the times in which the events of the book are set placed individuals on all sides under extraordinary – indeed, superhuman – pressures which resulted in sudden, and sometimes inexplicable, actions: 'When humans are brave, when they offer shelter, they don't always know exactly why, and those they help are often too desperate and terrorised at the time to ask why' (TP p.vi).

There are problems here. We may readily accept the account of (the real) Oskar's character which Keneally gives here but still feel unsatisfied with a fictional rendering dependent upon an account which is (in *fictional* terms) so incomplete: our dissatisfaction is not with Oskar as human protagonist, but with Keneally as literary craftsman. Keneally is correct to assert, albeit somewhat defensively, that 'you can't merely reduce the essential mystery of a human's nature and motives to figures', but in going on to say that 'Sometimes all you can do is to present the enigma' and that it was this he 'enjoyed trying to do with the Schindler story' he blurs distinctions proper to make in the response to a work of *fiction* between the raw material of the work (Shakespeare's sources for his figure of Hamlet, say) and the text we engage with. Shakespeare's feelings as he wrote the play are not known to us, and would be irrelevant – if intriguing – if they were.

A predictable response to these problems has been that *Schindler's Ark* is not a work of fiction at all, but of fact. An article in the *Daily Express* for October 1982 quoted Keneally himself on this topic as follows:

'Perhaps you could call it non-fiction fiction. I've moulded the material as you would for a novel – highlighting dramatic episodes, building up characterisation. But about a third of the way through, when the pace starts to hot up, the book becomes far more documentary than novel.' (TP p.345)

Other articles and reviews in Britain over the next few months referred confusingly to Keneally using his skills 'to re-create, rather than invent', to the idea of the 'non-fiction novel' being 'nonsense and an insult to fiction writers', to the book advancing 'the cause of the documentary novel' and to it being variously 'a highly competent piece of reportage' and 'imaginative historical journalism' (TP p.345). Confronted with such disagreement between the experts, the reader can have little hope (no more the present writer) of reaching any clear position. Keneally himself remains largely untroubled by such disputes within what he would no doubt see as academic literary criticism, observing with seemingly straightforward practicality:

> There was something in Schindler's character I did not want to deal with in biographical form.
> He hardly belonged to real life. He was so exotic, so complex, such a paradox, that he seemed to be part and parcel of a novel. (TP p.347)

In his Introduction to the *Textplus* edition, Keneally stresses that 'there was ambiguity in Schindler's story, and ambiguity is the bread and butter of the novelist', musing on the extent to which central characters may be compared and contrasted. 'Amon and Oskar (in this, too, Oskar's story is like fiction) were in fact very close temperamentally, two sides of the same being. Amon was the berserk killer, Oskar the berserk rescuer.' It is worth observing here that life resembles art to the extent (and no more) that we seek, and find, art-like patterns in it: all lives are 'like' fiction in this respect, not just Oskar's. We have seen that as a writer Keneally is irresistibly drawn to certain kinds of characters and themes, but it is possible to grant this as his personal way of working without conceding that Oskar's life was especially 'like fiction'. Was Hitler's, or Churchill's, or Mussolini's – or, indeed, Keneally's own earlier life – in this sense any more, or less, 'like fiction' than Oskar's? Even if we accept the contentious suggestion that characters in novels are more exotic, complex and paradoxical than characters in real life, the question remains unanswerable, not because we lack the relevant information but because it doesn't make sense; an answer is only possible when we have a particular historical study, biography or work of fiction to discuss. Until then, all human lives have the inherent possibility of 'artistic' shape and purpose – depending always upon the skill of the individual artist. It is especially relevant in the context of this novel to recall here that a religious view sees each individual life as possessing form and purpose as part of the divinely-sanctioned design. It would have been Keneally's responsibility to promulgate the truth of just such a design (in his case that of Catholicism) had he entered the priesthood; we might therefore ask what he means by claiming Schindler 'hardly belonged to real life', but seemed rather 'to be part and parcel of a novel'.

The shape and purpose Keneally attributes to Schindler's life is more properly seen as part of *authorial* focus and intention; after all, the mass of material that covered Keneally's pool table at Bilgola for all those months was 'arranged and coded with colour markers' precisely so that *he* might give it the shape it otherwise lacked. In this respect, Keneally underplays the contribution that an author makes in shaping the material of fiction, suggesting that such shape is found in life itself; yet form, like beauty, lies inevitably in the eye of the beholder, and it is that eye for form which is the essence of the artist. As John Berger expresses it:

> If Keneally found in Oskar's story 'the qualities and excitements of fiction' and in Oskar's life a shape 'which makes it very appropriate for a novelist to write about it', those things in themselves cannot make *Schindler's Ark* a novel. That must lie in the craft of the novelist – or, perhaps, in the decision of the publisher! (TP pp.327–8)

On another level, though, the role Keneally implies for the writer in discussing Schindler's story is daunting, for if indeed the novelist's duty is to transcribe – rather than imaginatively *de*scribe – the pre-existing shape such an unusual life possesses, then that writer indeed bears the responsibility of speaking for 'a thousand eyewitnesses who forgot nothing'. The problem, in the case of *Schindler's Ark*, is that the writer was not there. This uncomfortable juxtaposition of claimed historical authenticity and actual historical absence provides the context for a concluding discussion of Keneally's own contribution to the debate on his fiction.

Critics may prefer authors who write books but keep quiet; each party then has a defined role, though writers understandably can tend to see critics as somewhat parasitic. Many authors, though, enjoy debate on their works and, not surprisingly, often contribute to it with great articulacy. It is wise to be attentive yet sceptical when writers or artists talk of their own work. In one sense they are omniscient about its origins and techniques: the only source. In other ways, though, they are too close to the work, too intimately involved with its genesis and (often painful) gestation to have any special claim to critical objectivity in respect of the finished product. Their comments may satisfy our curiosity, but not always enhance our understanding; a work once published is, as the very term suggests, public critical property over which its creator has no special claim. Like children, books come to have lives of their own, no matter that their begetters may sometimes fondly wish otherwise.

Keneally's general position here, and certainly with regard to *Schindler's Ark*, is complicated. The account he provides of the book's origins is intriguing – thrilling even; occasionally, as I have argued, it reads like one of his own novels, and this may lead us to wonder whether it is (only) as factual as the book itself is, using 'the texture and devices of a novel to tell a true story' (TP p.vii). But if Keneally is apparently very forthcoming in furnishing contextual information, he is decidedly reticent on issues for which the novelist might reasonably be expected to shoulder responsibility, and defers always to the truth of the tale: 'I have attempted to avoid all fiction . . . since fiction would debase the record' (TP p.vii). This is an unhelpful blurring between the unavoidable use of fictional devices (such as narrative and character) in relating historical events and what Keneally terms the use of 'the texture and devices of a novel to tell a true story' (TP p.vii). It is also a blurring which some commentators have felt damage, rather than enhance, the book.

One reviewer who questioned Keneally's success in telling a true story was Peter Gilbert in *The Jewish Chronicle*, who felt that 'however efficient and professional the style is, it seems to lack the grain of experienced reality' and that 'there are limitations to what the book has achieved, which follow directly from Keneally having chosen to write it as a faction'. Gilbert instances the extent to which Schindler's 'inner life remains shadowy', and observes:

> Had the book been written as a novel based on the story of Oskar Schindler, Keneally would perhaps have felt greater freedom to enlarge on his hero's character, to recreate it from within, so to speak, and possibly would have made him more understandable. Had he chosen to write a straightforward biography he would at least then have had to attempt to explain the mystery of why Schindler acted as he did. As it is, the book falls somewhat between two stools. . . . (TP p.352)

This chapter opened with a quotation from an essay on literature and history by the distinguished St Lucian poet Derek Walcott (b.1930).

a writer whose sharp awareness of the cruel and complex history of the Caribbean since it was colonised by European countries – Britain, France, Spain, Holland – makes him especially concerned with the relationship between literature and history. It also makes him alert to the authorship of literary or historical works for if – as he argues – memory, invention and myth shape both, then the nationality, race, culture and gender of the writer will inevitably shape their writing. To suggest otherwise would be to cast the authors not as 'objective', but as less than human.

As a black writer from a part of the world whose history has been written almost exclusively by others (often by overseas experts whose countrymen were earlier responsible for the process of colonisation and slavery) Walcott sees 'history' as a far more problematic concept than does Keneally. It is true that in his own historical works, including those set in Australia, Keneally does focus on victims rather than heroes, in Walcott's terms, but there is no sense that he questions – or is even interested in – the complex relationships between written and oral records, memory and imagination, in the *writing* of history. Above all, the relish with which Keneally sees history as a repository of ready-shaped epochs and characters with which to people his fiction sweeps aside any consideration of the problems inherent in reliance on historical authorities, problems which Walcott expresses by terming history 'a kind of literature without morality'.

The concept of morality is crucial here, a notion with which Keneally's reference to history as containing 'parables' for the present presumably signals his general agreement. For Walcott history lacks the morality that literature possesses precisely because it claims to be objective, to relate 'facts'. He is not here denying that certain events took place – the wars in The Falklands and the Gulf certainly did – but pointing out that scholarly historians from Argentina, Britain, Iran, Jordan and the United States (say) might reasonably be expected to give differing accounts of the causes, progress and conclusion of hostilities. Even within Britain historians, like other individuals, will vary in their opinions according to politics, race, religion – and many other factors, all of them complex and unpredictable.

Clearly such a vision of history makes it at best a problematic source for those parables which attract Keneally, and also suggests that if we feel our debt to historians to be 'beyond estimation' then that may well be because a particular rendering of the facts accords with interests and preferences of our own. As for Keneally's claim that he sought to avoid all fiction in *Schindler's Ark* 'since fiction would debase the record', the very point of Walcott's contention is that any 'record' that claims objectivity is at best naive, at worst dishonest. The best documentary films (to make comparison with a medium which Keneally himself has seen as more important today than the novel), are not those which claim to be objective but those which are open in their commitment to uncovering injustice or suffering. For the historian, of course, such an argument raises thorny problems: how *does* one write 'objectively' about, say, the 400 years of slavery of which Bob Marley sings, and from which Britain prospered massively until its abolition in 1837? And how convincing can it be for an historian writing on this topic to claim that his or her colour is irrelevant to the 'scholarly research' in the book?

Keneally's own preference has always been for 'history' to be focused in a particular personality or a sharply-defined series of events: all the books discussed here confirm this, as would his portrayal of Joan of Arc in *Blood Red, Sister Rose*, of the First World War period in *Gossip from the Forest* and of aspects of the Pacific war in *The Cut-Rate Kingdom*. Such personalities have also, as we have seen, tended to be remote in both space and time from his own. The effect of this preference, and it may well also be the reason, is that it absolves the author from the need to engage with those very issues to which Walcott's analysis directs our attention. A further effect of this focus on personality rather than process is, ironically, that the personalities themselves often seem 'shadowy' – to use Peter Gilbert's term – since the author can never draw back to show the wider scene in all its truly historical scope and complexity. Aside from some directives from the upper echelons of the Nazi administration, how much of an impression (let alone a picture) does the reader gain of the political and economic period in which Schindler operates? Both the politics and the economics are strictly local and personal: for example, the horrific scene in which Oskar plays cards with Amon Goth, the camp commandant, the stakes being the right of the Jewish prisoner Helen Hirsch to be on the Schindler list for 'relocation' (Ch.30). The scene is so horrific chiefly because such a game of cards *did* take place, but the large and the small events of history unfold from just such trivial decisions – or indecisions. The imbalance in Keneally's view of history is that while he promises unremittingly truthful access to a particular period we sometimes come away with little more than tourist curios; such disappointment is the price we pay for the Faustian excitement of witnessing history 'in the flesh'.

Readers will react differently to *Schindler's Ark*, but whatever their assessment of it, a decision on whether to accept it as the 'non-fiction fiction' Keneally suggested it was – and an understanding of what this description might mean – must preface debate. To the extent that Keneally has constructed an ambiguous status for the book, albeit for what he genuinely sees as important reasons, he may yet prove to have been the most troublesome commentator on this extraordinary work.

6

The Bookmaker: *The Playmaker*

The society that had produced us [in Tasmania], so far away from what it saw as the centre of civilisation, made us rather like the prisoners in Plato's cave. To guess what the centre was like, that centre 12,000 miles away for which we yearned, we must study shadows on the wall. . . .
(Christopher Koch, 'The Lost Hemisphere' in *Crossing the Gap: A Novelist's Essays*, 1987)

Antibiotics and plumbing have made melodrama laughable to the modern reader. . . . The Sichuanese, the Eritreans or the Masai would understand better than us the destinies which befell some of our players and in particular our playmaker, Lieutenant Ralph Clark.
   For yes, though they are fantastical creatures, they all lived.
(from the Epilogue to *The Playmaker*, 1987)

Melodrama: a dramatic piece characterised by sensational incident and violent appeals to the emotions, but with a happy ending.
(*The Oxford Companion to English Literature*)

It will be clear from the interests and approaches explored in this study that for Thomas Keneally 1988 would be a crucial year: it marked 200 years of white settlement at 'the world's worst end' and offered him a unique opportunity to 'celebrate' the occasion in the full sense not only of rejoicing, but also of observing, performing and proclaiming. It was unthinkable that Keneally would not produce a new book for the Bicentennial (Patrick White made it clear, by contrast, that he certainly would not), and in *The Playmaker* he delivered a work which offered a mixture of sex, violence and symbolism heady enough to satisfy the most demanding critic. More than that, it can be seen as the book in

which he most completely realised the role of author which is variously
implicit in all his works, that of the hidden but all-controlling creator.
In *The Playmaker* the power of this figure is no longer suggested
through images of a magnified vision of the human battlefield (as
in *Confederates*) or a distant witnessing of violent action (as in
Schindler's Ark) but finds direct embodiment in the complex image
not of play-actor, not of play director, but of 'playmaker'.

In constructing this image of his own country's early years Keneally
turns again to those times and traits which he had explored twenty
years before in *Bring Larks and Heroes*: the ironies of colonial
life as a cruel parody of English manners and *mores*; the unique
isolation in time and space of New South Wales; the necessity,
notwithstanding, for human aspirations – noble and base alike –
to be satisfied. Much of the atmosphere and incident of this book
echoes that of the earlier novel, but Keneally's playmaker image places
these in a very different light, especially so because – with almost
self-parodying daring – the novel employs a series of complementing
and mutually-reflexive 'playmaker' personae: the English dramatist
George Farquhar (1678–1707), whose play *The Recruiting Officer*
was first performed at London's Drury Lane in April, 1706; Lieutenant
Ralph Clark, producing Farquhar's play to honour the King's birthday
in June, 1789; and, by no means least, one Thomas Keneally, plotting
everything from behind these multi-layered sets. In tone, too, this
book is very different, for the licence of the theatrical world – its
auditions, readings, make-up and dressing up – offer rich possibilities
not only for that interpenetration of different worlds that Keneally
loves but also, as the opening quotation makes clear, of a true
melodrama of life. Keneally himself has compared it to a scathing (and
hilarious) 1971 political and social satire by the Australian dramatist
David Williamson: 'It's the 18th century *Don's Party* [the title of
Williamson's play] . . . highly recommended as midnight reading for
closet sexists everywhere'.[1]

Recent works by Keneally have consistently led the reader into the
text through a series of factual signposts: maps, notes, authorial notes
and evocative acknowledgements and dedications. He concluded his
Bibliographical Note at the end of *Confederates* with the strangely
imperious (almost Papal) benediction: 'May all these authors, the
living and the dead, flourish in reputation'. Some ten years later

---

1. Bob Ellis, 'Thomas Keneally: The Wizard of Oz Lit', *Times on Sunday* (Australia),
11 October 1987, pp.25–6. Reference on p.25. I am grateful to Katherine Gallagher
for this reference.

our approach to *The Playmaker* (it is not flagged as a novel) is via a dedication to 'Arabanoo' – an Aboriginal who also features in the book – 'and his brethren, still dispossessed'; an Author's Note on historical sources; a 'playbill' for Lieutenant Clark's production and a list of 'Dramatis Personae'. Finally, we have a 'factual' explanation of 'The Players', listing their origins, crimes, sentences and ages.

Thus far the book might indeed seem to promise the 'rollocking (sic) thoughtful tale', the 'lusty and affectionate tribute to Australia's raw beginnings', that the *Publishers Weekly* (quoted inside the cover) apparently saw. That Keneally had rather more complex aims is, however, suggested by the quotation above, which comes from what Keneally presents as the largely-factual Epilogue to the book (this, like the last chapter of *Confederates*, does what it can to conclude the lives of the 'characters' whose actions we have followed). The relevance of their intertwining stories lies as much in the casual coincidence Keneally perceives – or attributes – as in any quality of their 'Australianness'. To see *The Playmaker* as a work deeply Australian, and not only in its subject matter, is an essential preliminary step; to see it as only concerned with colonial Australia is to misunderstand Keneally's intentions. The text opens with images which emphasise not a close focus on Australia but rather the sense in which the new colony – 'this new penal planet' – is a world whose self-contained and distant quality makes it particular in detail but universal in significance: for Ralph Clark the colony is 'two years in time and eight months travel in space' distant from his wife in Plymouth, and it is the suggestion that it offers an historically-rooted understanding of the present-day third world that locates this book in the mainstream of Keneally's output over the past thirty years. Throughout the book a double focus is employed, an overlapping vision which both images and reflects the disjunction inherent in the very nature of 'this outermost penal station of the universe': it defies comparison with other settlements in the civilised world while it mimics their selfsame qualities:

> This penal station had the literal appearance of a town because of its peculiar circumstances. There were no walls or compounds – space and distance and time were the walls and the compound. So, like London, Paris, Vienna and any other settlement marked by the European genius the town had already developed quarters and suburbs – a fashionable and a rough side. (Ch.2)

With space and distance as town walls, the settlement is well placed to be seen as truly universal in its mythological significance. Another way in which the text gestures towards universality is through the selection process by which this particular play came to be produced at this time and place: there was no selection process, since 'in all this vast reach of the universe it was the one play of which two copies existed: There was Lieutenant George Johnston's copy, and Captain Davy Collins's copy' (Ch.1). Everything is both ordained and casual, planned and random: so, too, Keneally the bookmaker muses on the 'lifestory' pattern of his players: 'Of them fiction could make much, though history says nothing' (Epilogue). Here, the plot – not of the play to be produced, but of the novel about its production – is presented by Keneally as something given rather than decided; once again he demonstrates his preference for a basic pattern to be laid down, within which fiction can operate. In *The Playmaker* we are invited to accept the events as having special significance by virtue of their being acted out on 'the first primitive stage of this new earth' (Ch.1).

Ralph, the playmaker of the title, is presented by Keneally as an individual whose authority derives not only from his modest status within the forces of order, but also from the power he acquires through the dramatic production itself; indeed, there are occasions on which the priority status of his production (in celebration of the King's birthday) enables Ralph to fend off legal claims on his would-be actors. The need to rehearse parts in one play precludes the acting out of other dramas in the courtroom – if not on the scaffold (at least for a time).

At least since *As You Like It* we have known that 'all the world's a stage', and that 'one man in his time plays many parts': Keneally gambles in deciding to foreground such a well-worn image (so well-worn as to be a cliché) in the very structure of his book. To suggest that the life of Oskar Schindler mirrored the structures of fiction was unusual – even faintly shocking, given the context – but this comparison is positively creaky in its obviousness. How so? Keneally's riposte is that the obviousness, the farce, the crudeness of characterisation and plot in his book only appear so because our modern perspective has been distorted by 'antibiotics and plumbing'. He emphasises, too, that the player in his book with the most extraordinary destiny is the playmaker himself, Lieutenant Ralph Clark, who invented a new life for himself on the penal planet of Australia and who – when he and his official family expired in different places but in a single 'pulse of time' – was survived only by 'his lag-wife Brenham and the new world child Alicia'. That this child – this new Eve – is named after his old-world wife completes Keneally's intriguing circle of art and life.

Such satisfaction for the reader, as well as the author, is pitched, though, against the ever-pressing reminders of death and corruption;

this is the raw material out of which the performance comes, the fiction is wrought: 'It seemed that all the cove was engaged in tedium and the remembrance of mortality' (Ch.3). Convict Mary Brenham — the playmaker's 'lag-wife' to be — copies 'the living words of George Farquhar' (Ch.3), and in responding to the magic of language, invention and imagination she and her fellows (the official dregs of so-called civilised society) demonstrate their shared humanity with those who are cast in the roles of their masters in 'this strange reach of the universe' (Ch.4).

It would seem, looking at *The Playmaker* in the light of Keneally's earlier writings, that this return to Australia as a literary stage for acting out his own preoccupations was little short of inevitable; the period demonstrates too dramatically — melodramatically, even — the images central to his view of the world for him to be able to stay away from it for long. Above all, it is the essential contradictions of the place that fascinate. Some who came to Australia (we learn by looking over Captain Davy Collins's shoulder, as he writes his journal) had been 'taken in by the repute the earliest visitors, James Cook, his artists and his scientists, had — some eighteen years before — given the place', but Keneally's own vision stresses the antitheses that some commentators attributed to the Antipodes:

> It was not concerned with entertaining people. Its dun forests affronted them, its vivid birds shrieked and were inedible, its beasts mocked the Ark. Its Indians lived by rules further removed than the stars from the normal rules of humankind. (Ch.4)

The best-known expression of such a view of Australia as everything opposite and disturbing to a 'normal' (European) sensibility is the Preface by the novelist Marcus Clarke to Adam Lindsay Gordon's *Poems* (1876); both writers were born into wealthy English families, and went to Australia in their twenties (in time-honoured tradition) to make good their lost fortunes:

> What is the dominant note of Australian scenery? That which is the dominant note of Edgar Allan Poe's poetry — Weird Melancholy.
> . . .
> Australia has rightly been named the Land of the Dawning. Wrapped in the midst of early morning, her history looms vague and gigantic. The lonely horseman riding between the moonlight and the day sees vast shadows creeping across the shelterless and silent plains, hears strange noises in the primeval forest, where flourishes a vegetation long dead in other lands, and feels, despite his fortune, that the trim

utilitarian civilisation which bred him shrinks into significance beside the contemptuous grandeur of forest and ranges coeval with an age in which European scientists have cradled his race.[2]

This extensive quotation bears remarkable similarity to descriptions of Australia as almost another planet in *The Playmaker* (and, earlier, in *Bring Larks and Heroes*), but as Clarke's reference to Poe reveals, such attitudes owed as much to a certain literary sensibility (itself shaped by some very un-Australian influences) as to any actual characteristics of Australian scenery. The same is true, of course, of *any* attitude to, or definition of, 'Australia': 'there is no unmediated access to reality, either through perception or through memory'.[3] What is of interest is the extent to which Keneally's vision of his homeland – a vision that many Australians today would find decidedly odd – resembles that of an earlier period, and exercises such power for him.

'A fool sees not the same tree that a wise man sees,' wrote the English poet William Blake. Recognition of such individuality of character is central to Keneally's writing, yet he tends towards a stereotypical vision of Australia. What is constant is that sense of Australia as a place indifferent, if not inimical, to any human presence, and this attitude is presented in *The Playmaker* not as the opinion of 'ordinary commissioned oafs like Lieutenant Faddy and Captain Meredith' but as the more realistic, the more demanding, assessment of the place: 'It was the anti-Europe. You needed a subtle mind if you were to find wonders here once a month let alone daily' (Ch.4).

This perspective of watching distorted shadows of reality on the wall is exactly that described by the Tasmanian writer Christopher Koch (born 1932) in the quotation that heads this chapter. Koch's own father was German, but his son – 'like many another child of the Empire in the Thirties' – was named after A.A. Milne's Christopher Robin. The experiences Koch charts in his perceptive collection of essays closely parallel those of Keneally, and Tasmanians (whose very island sometimes drops off maps of Australia) are especially sensitive to

2. Marcus Clarke, Preface to Gordon's *Poems*, 1876; in the excellent collection edited by John Barnes, *The Writer in Australia: A Collection of Literary Documents 1856–1964* (Oxford University Press, 1969), pp.33–7. Reference on p.35.
3. Coral Ann Howells, *Private and Fictional Words: Canadian Women Novelists of the 1970s and 1980s* (Methuen, 1987), p.45. Howells's book is a stimulating study – by an Australian who teaches in Britain – and addresses many issues of fiction and history relevant also to Keneally's writing:

> Only through story-telling can connections with the past be realised, for inheritance comes to possess reality only when it is re-imagined and when history and legend are so closely interwoven that no objective truth is possible. (p.21)

questions of centres and peripheries; for them, Sydney or Melbourne is already an overseas 'centre', from which their homeland is perceived as correspondingly 'other'.

On his own admission, and his fiction makes it equally clear, Keneally has never been able to feel totally at home in Australia, at least not in his capacity as creative artist. In this sense the glimpse he gives of writing *Schindler's Ark* in the 'so-called office under my house at Bilgola Beach in Sydney' with all the material spread out on his pool table and 'coded with coloured markers' appears emblematic of his physical location, yet imaginative dislocation, in Australia. We can sense the excitement here – even in retrospect – and such planning and coding (in whatever form) is often very much part of the creative process; we should not underestimate its importance. What seems distinctive about Keneally's sense of excitement is that special *frisson* he derives from the contrast and distance of which he is so aware.

With a similar background, Christopher Koch drew on his own time abroad to write a fine 1978 novel set in Indonesia (*The Year of Living Dangerously*; filmed by Peter Weir in 1982). He has also suggested, in his essay 'Asia and the Australian Imagination' in *Crossing the Gap*, that there are real analogies between Australia and what (in imperial geography) was 'the Far East' (Australia's near-North): 'With Indonesia, in particular, we in Australia have a future to invent together. . . . The future we face in the Pacific may be dangerous, but I suspect it will be anything but dull.' Such a comment highlights how little Keneally's writings have to offer on Australia's role as a Pacific nation (*The Cut-Rate Kingdom* was more concerned with Australia's relationship with the United States); his consistent concern is with the older links of British imperial history, with history altogether 'other' (France; America; Germany) or – pervasively if indirectly – with his own personal and spiritual history.

The Playmaker is dedicated 'To Arabanoo and his brethren, still dispossessed', while at the very end of the 'Epilogue' Keneally comments of the convict 'players' in the drama we have followed: 'Of them fiction could make much, though history says nothing'. The claim of the book, then, both in its dedication and in its closing words, is to speak for those about whose fate history is silent or indifferent – or both; people whom the Australian poet Bruce Dawe once termed 'those in our midst for whom no-one speaks, and who cannot speak for themselves'. In its entirety the book does indeed 'make much' of those oppressed individuals who, if they feature at all in history, feature only as the illiterate raw material of problematic statistics in ledgers kept by their masters. That said, it remains unclear how either the heritage or the subsequent history of Arabanoo and his brethren is relevant to those whose hopes and fears we follow in *The Playmaker*; hangman, whore or play director, they all in their different ways contribute to Arabanoo's dispossession. The appearance of Arabanoo, after his capture, as His Excellency's pet native at rehearsals for Ralph's play seems to confirm as tenuous any link between these two strands of the plot: there is an immediate theatricality about the confrontation which Keneally responds to with typical liveliness and wit:

> Arabanoo seemed to take some comfort from the rehearsals. It was possible, thought Ralph, that he considered the reading of the lines and the rehearsal of actions to have religious meaning, and Ralph was beginning to wonder himself if it were not so.
>
> Arabanoo was captured on the lag city's first new year's eve in the middle of the previous summer. Or, as H.E. looked on it, he was rescued, taken out of his *ab origine* timelessness and introduced to breeches and naval jacket and the Gregorian calendar. (Ch.14)

This is a sharply-contrived image of culture-contact, and of the gruesomely unintentional humour of dispossession: we take the point that Arabanoo is dressed up by his masters to learn and play a part for real. There seems no intrinsic link beyond this image, though, and such reference to parts and players is itself but one more instance of the underlying image of the whole book. As for Ralph 'beginning to wonder' whether his play has religious significance, wonder he may – and we with him – but the suggestions floats, unrelated and unsubstantiated, more as mystification than mystery.

One mystery that Keneally's writing shows to be of endless fascination for him, but which – rather surprisingly, given the opportunities – he touches on little in this book is that of the impenetrability of flesh and bone to intellectual speculation. The hangman, Ketch Freeman, is shunned by the other convicts for his gruesome role, but Keneally's curiosity takes us also to the grim aftermath, on the autopsy table, of a passionate murder among the soldiers, and ensures that the two surgeons, by virtue of their need to explain procedure to official witnesses Ralph and Harry, spare the reader few details:

> Johnny White said, 'I intend to open the cranium, and although that will not be too horrific, I would understand if you wished to wait outside.'

> Yet both Ralph and Harry stayed – Ralph out of a sort of military pride, Harry perhaps from a desire to see Handy Baker's malice made visible beneath Bullmore's skull.
>
> . . .
>
> . . . Having cut a clean inverted dish of bone off the top of Bullmore's cranium, he removed that shield to expose what he called the *Dura Mater*, which he now began to probe with scissors. (Ch.12)

It is in such scenes that Keneally seems closest to the trans-substantial mystery most absorbing to him, but its fascination is also its most frustrating aspect; it reveals nothing, leaving life – and death – as banal and baffling as ever:

> 'You can say, Harry, that there is a quantity of extravasated blood under the skull and between the *Dura* and *Pia Mater* on the occiput or hinder part of the head. This was caused by blows or a heavy fall and was on its own enough to kill the boy.' (Ch.12)

The intimate and the physical, flesh in all its desirability and decay, always draws Keneally's attention as inevitably as it leaves him both properly mystified and obscurely uneasy. Sexual intercourse is rarely represented by Keneally as anything other than a physical, and largely violent, act: 'There, on a pallet, the big Marine, Private Handy Baker, dressed in a shirt, was plunging and rearing between Duckling's knees' (Ch.24). And just as in *Schindler's Ark* the European political and financial scene is reduced to Oskar's intrigues to save his workers (and the black marketeering this entails) so in *The Playmaker* the very concept of money shrinks to very immediate terms:

> At this penal reach of the universe there *was* no real entity called money. Money was Liz Barber's thighs. Money was wine, money was spirits. Money was flour Black Caesar had absconded with. Money was edible, potable, solid. Whereas a sum like seventy-six pounds eleven shillings and sixpence seemed a chimera. (Ch.19)

Such a passage points to the strengths of this book: a vivid and energetic evocation of setting and personality, but also to its shortcomings. Despite the cleverly-contrived fabric of the 'drama', the overall impression is of sharply-outlined but essentially two-dimensional 'characters' being manoeuvred all too obviously by Keneally the 'bookmaker'. Where physical settings and events are evoked in a fairly straightforward manner the result is successful; attempts to make them bear more complex significance are less so. Perhaps the most climactically risible – certainly melodramatic – incident is that in which play director Ralph finally consummates his passion for actress Mary Brenham (the reader needs to know that she is deeply ashamed of a strategically located tattoo . . .):

> What exquisite gasps compounded of Farquhar and unhappy criminality, of what Ralph thought of as lost years and unchosen motherhood, went into her cry as he entered. When he turned her over it was because he wished to demonstrate to her, at the peak of his joy, that her tattooed arse meant nothing. Raging as he gave himself, he saw the calligraphy of her thirteen-year-old folly shining like some runic inscription. (Ch.27)

The kindest critical assessment of this key passage – the bearer of the tattoo will become Ralph's lag wife – is that it clearly indicates Keneally's talents to lie elsewhere.

In the final chapter of the book Lieutenant Ralph Clark muses during the production of his play on its nature and effect. It is clearly a passage crucial to Keneally's artistic aims with *his* players, but the lasting effect is of wooden and slightly self-conscious explication to the reader (lest we miss the point?) rather than any rewarding enrichment of our response to the text:

> He had a sense that his players had somehow become their own actors, independent of him like grown children, that he was no longer bound to them by either pleasure or duty, that they had entered into a pact with the audience which was rightly none of his business and that only the approval of the crowd could justify them and assure the maturity of their craft. (Ch.30)

As anyone who has directed or acted in plays will know, the realistic structures here are at odds with symbolic: it is the authorial contrivance of Keneally, not the suggested 'child-maturity' dynamic of Ralph's production, that dominates.

The significance of *The Playmaker* within the spectrum of Keneally's works lies more in the understanding it provides of Keneally's approaches to fiction and to character than in any outstanding literary merit. It was a fitting offering in Bicentennial year, and has all the spirit of a festive offering, not forgetting the timely, if somewhat extraneous, inclusion of Aboriginal peoples and their part in the unfolding drama that would be Australia. Like play director Ralph, we watch 'his creatures come and go on the bright stage' (Ch.30) and there is real delight in the vividness with which Keneally controls *his* creatures through their parts. If the deeper significances that Keneally hints at, and Ralph muses on, remain unrealised in artistic terms, perhaps we – like Ralph – should rejoice in the more modest but immensely enjoyable events of the moment-to-moment drama: 'They were locked for the rest of the day in their characters. This gratified Ralph the playmaker who would have been tempted – if he had the power – to keep them like this for ever' (Ch.30).

7

Conclusion

Most new nations go through the formality of inventing a national identity, but Australia has long supported a whole industry of image-makers to tell us what we are. Throughout its white history, there have been countless attempts to get Australia down on paper and to catch its essence. Their aim is not merely to describe the continent, but to give it an individuality, a personality. This they call Australia, but it is more likely to reflect the hopes, fears or needs of its inventor.
(Richard White, *Inventing Australia: Images and Identity 1688–1980*, 1981)

For Irish Catholics of my generation, doing time in a seminary was rather like doing your national service.
(Thomas Keneally, quoted by William Foster, Textplus edition of *Schindler's Ark*, 1982)

These two quotations express general and personal versions of what are, in effect, two very different 'Australias'. White's comment directs our attention away from arguing whether a particular definition of Australia is 'right' or 'wrong' and towards considering why it should have been held at a particular period. This is the most fruitful approach to Keneally's rendering of history, not research into, or quibbling about, whether particular details of this or that rendering are correct or not (some will almost certainly be wrong).

This approach to history is scholarly and detached, very different from that of the individual who may well be concerned much with immediate conditions, the position from which Keneally's comment is made. His almost dismissive comment about the seven or so years he spent 'doing time' in a seminary suggests that this was simply part of growing up, something that everyone – or at least, all Irish Catholic

Australians – did. Having missed National Service in Britain by one year, and writing as a lifelong agnostic, I have no exact personal analogy to draw upon, but consideration of Keneally's writing suggests that the preoccupations that led him to study for the priesthood, like the doubts that led him eventually to opt for the secular life some thirty years ago, have left their mark. It would be strange if it were otherwise; the years between the mid-teens and the mid-twenties are formative for most of us, and though Keneally's comparison with National Service may be half-joking, the implied reference to compulsion, discipline, suffering and self-denial is exact (and is confirmed by the recurrence of such themes in his fiction).

Two helpful analogies for the time Keneally spent in his seminary are those of the art of history and the art of fiction: both offer us a shape and order for experience which must otherwise by chaotic, devoid of meaning. Placing these two 'arts' together in this way of course raises consideration of the crucial differences that teachers and scholars in the respective fields see between them. In his writing, though, Keneally delights in eliding any notional boundary, bringing history 'alive' through the devices of the novelist while simultaneously foregrounding his factual sources and guarantees of historical truth. This Conclusion will suggest some ways of addressing Keneally's achievements and shortcomings as a writer, including the extent to which his position as an internationally successful *Australian* writer is relevant.

Finally, a warning: the reader should take to heart White's comments in considering the view of Keneally's work that follows: no doubt it, too, reflects the hopes, fears or needs of its author (as do all writings, whether they carry a health warning or not).

The themes chosen by Keneally for his most successful books parallel the reputation they have brought him: weighty, international and popular (in whatever order). Since he was institutionalised by the Booker Prize, reprints of earlier novels have carried the warranty: 'A novel by the author of *Schindler's Ark*'. Such are the ways of today's competitive publishing world, and Keneally, one imagines, would be the last to disapprove: he lives by his writing, and has been very successful both in reputation and earnings. The local boy has made good, materially and in the sense that, however much he may once have felt – or may still feel – 'alienated' in Australia, today he helps define Australia in the popular imagination, especially overseas. Yet this status has been achieved through works mostly set outside Australia, and comparison with the work of an Australian author such as Peter Carey, say – or, in a slightly earlier period, Patrick White – illustrates this striking difference.

Keneally's own comments, quoted in the Introduction to this study, remind us that such fame can be constricting for a writer, especially the national-specific emphasis it can encourage. With this in mind, what conclusions can, or should, we draw from the books themselves – and from critical discussion of Keneally – about his own aims and achievements as a writer? These basic questions have not often been addressed because of the nature of Keneally's work and the response it encourages from commentators. Even today, almost all the serious critical work on Keneally is done in Australian literary journals, a somewhat surprising fact which contrasts strongly with his high international profile. A work such as *The Playmaker* is praised on the back cover by David Hughes in *The Mail on Sunday* as a 'magnificent and moving documentary' which is 'a tribute to his roots', but as we saw in the Introduction to this study, Keneally's 'roots' are more complicated than this comment suggests – as, indeed, is the status of the book itself as 'documentary' (not something claimed by the author).

Keneally himself has said that his work has always been reviewed more favourably in Britain than in Australia, but many British reviews do fall into a weekend style of 'sound bites' which recycle accepted Keneally adjectives – 'strong', 'brilliant', 'extraordinary' and 'moving'. Taken together these are not terms which advance debate, or enhance our understanding of Keneally's strengths and weaknesses as a writer; indeed, his seeming preference for the 'extraordinary' in his writing may not necessarily be the virtue reviewers assume. British reviewers often seem to praise Keneally for just that strange and exotic quality (as they see it) that his complex adjustments to his own Australian background might be expected to have made him keen to avoid. For example, comparisons were understandably made between *The Playmaker* and Robert Hughes's popular study (important partly because it is so readable) of Australia's convict period, *The Fatal Shore*, published late the previous year. It was Hughes, though, who in an earlier critical history, *The Art of Australia* (1966) made some sharp, but highly relevant, observations on the character of Australian culture. Hughes first quoted a general assessment of Australian art by another Australian writer and critic, Craig McGregor:

> Australians tend to paint in a direct, unselfconscious way, unworried by too great an acquaintance with self-debilitating doubts and the metaphysics of many overseas artists; the result is a certain bravura and confidence, a readiness to grapple with the major theme and to make the large statement ... there is a breadth and yet an innocence about much Australian painting. ...

This might well seem a passage only too exact for a consideration of Keneally's work; certainly it would not be out of place in many critical reviews. Hughes commented drily on the assessment as follows:

> The truth is nearly exactly the opposite. Australian painting is very self-conscious; it is obsessed with the problem of what its identity ought to be. To be free from doubt and indifferent to 'metaphysics' – by which, presumably, the author means 'aesthetics' – is not necessarily praiseworthy in artists. The 'readiness to grapple with major themes' (in a state of 'innocence', perverse as that may seem) and the fondness for 'large statements' (for which, all too often, one has only to thank the mills which supply Masonite [a composite board] in 6 × 4 sheets) are often nothing more than masks for the existing doubt.

Hughes does grant that 'Australians are certainly fond of heroic themes', but adds that 'all their heroes are pre-Freudian' and, more generally, that 'innocence can be one of the faces of rhetoric'.[1] His remarks are 25 years old (they coincide with publication of *Bring Larks and Heroes*) but their freshness – and relevance – remain. Some Australian critical work on Keneally has tackled similar considerations with regard to his fiction, but until overseas critics become similarly incisive it would seem that Keneally must look to his 'roots' for the most illuminating, if not always the most complimentary, criticism:

> Keneally ... regards himself as a mediator in the eschatological struggle. He venerates and translates what is authoritative, and he attempts to consecrate what he regards as mere form. He doesn't regard himself as a source or an authority. He once said 'order is beyond me' when referring to his research techniques, which is fortuitously emblematic of his total state of consciousness.[2]

In an immediate sense, the most outstanding quality of Keneally's writing remains its skilful integration of historical interest in event and setting with dramatic immediacy in characterisation and dialogue: it is also the quality which has continued to impress and to intrigue commentators. They consistently praise the 'faultless sense of place and period Keneally brings to life in memorable detail', claiming that 'only a writer of unusual talent would succeed in making such a moving parable' out of what one Australian critic termed (with reference to *Bring Larks and Heroes*) 'our heritage of cruelty'. Throughout critical

1. Robert Hughes, *The Art of Australia* (Penguin, 1970), p.314.
2. English, 'History and the Refuge of Art', p.23.

comment on a range of works there is repeated reference to Keneally's 'triumph' in producing a 'moving documentary' through his 'audacity' and 'bravura' in a 'brilliantly detailed' treatment of 'historical persons and events'. These are, as we have seen, all terms which the author himself would welcome in describing his aims. Such an extraordinary coincidence of stated aims and perceived achievement is best explained by reference to Keneally's own persuasiveness and to a delicate and complex relationship between Keneally's own Australian past and the past of 'Western' popular imagination.

As the need for a readily available (and so necessarily largely undifferentiated) past increases the future seems ever more daunting, its most visible manifestation being the growth of nostalgia. This has advanced way beyond the 1950s, for long a convenient mid-century reference, and modern technology renders all things quickly obsolete – and therefore potentially collectable for what Keneally might term their 'reek and savour' of another time; 'collectables' is a new term in our language, alongside 'antiques', 'memorabilia' and 'bric-a-brac'. Antique dealers in Britain complain that the popular television programme the 'Antiques Roadshow', which tours the country inviting local people to have their possessions valued on-screen by experts, has ruined the professional trade: we all now wonder whether Auntie's vase, last seen among attic cobwebs, might be Ming. Complementary trends operate in the publicly-funded areas of conservation and heritage, while British farmers (who only recently were clearing hedgerows to introduce cost-effective 'agribusiness') are now told by the government that European Community production surpluses dictate a policy of looking to the 'farm holiday' market, and to tourist exploitation of such charming barns and quaint equipment as has survived. In the summer months buses with the sign 'Exeter Heritage Tours' drive slowly past my office on campus; the passengers look out dutifully at the university buildings. It seems that I, too, form part of some tourists' past. How do such instances of popular attitudes to different versions of the past relate to Thomas Keneally's writings? Most importantly, his books promise the reader easy and instant access to historical characters, and to a 'period feel' for the times they inhabit, across a wide historical and geographical range. Yet a curious feature of this past that we encounter so directly in the novels is that its inhabitants have more qualities in common than set them apart; Keneally has indeed the style of 'a thousand eyewitnesses who forgot nothing', and he travels wide and fast across varied historical terrain. The image of historical event as 'compelling science-fiction', which Keneally used in seeking to describe the enormity of the

Holocaust, is revealing here: it is as time-travellers that we visit the locales of Keneally's writing, our medium no time-machine but the author's personally-spun web of words.

Keneally's approach to the past relies on a fundamental blurring of difference between it and the present which far outweighs that replication of minor detail with which he seeks to evoke any specific place or period. As Robert Burns has argued, Keneally 'sees events and people in their categorical aspect', though, he suggests, 'the effect of this is not to subtract from their reality, in the main, but to heighten it (sometimes, it seems, beyond due bounds).'[3] As author, Keneally often places himself in the irreconcilable position of insisting that his recreated past can be trusted while at the same time positing himself and his authorial skills as the sole source of authority. The comments of Raymond Williams in *The Country and the City* (1973) on Oliver Goldsmith's poem 'The Deserted Village' (1769) – a work which Keneally recalled having studied at school – seem relevant here. Williams comments:

> The present is accurately and powerfully seen, but its real relations, to past and future, are inaccessible, because the governing development is that of the writer himself: a feeling about the past, an idea about the future, into which, by what is truly an intersection, an observed present is arranged.[4]

One would have to add, referring to Keneally, that it may equally well be the past that is 'intersected' into the present, but in his fiction his own development and feeling for the past is always a crucial consideration – and one that has been mostly ignored.

Not all critics, it is fair to say, have been impressed with Keneally's efforts to establish his fictional presents convincingly, and the Melbourne critic David English, in a most perceptive article, argues that Keneally:

> tends to behave as the omniscient repository of technical detail, terms, and incidental observations which are placed, almost precipitated, into the narrative, presumably to add authenticity. The effect, however, is often a voyeuristic fetishism; the calibre and names of guns, the branches and anabranches of rivers, the precise ranks and equivalents of officers of the S.S., compel in him an ambiguous boyish fascination.[5]

3. Robert Burns, 'A Study of Thomas Keneally's Novels', *Australian Literary Studies* (Brisbane) 4/1 May 1969, pp.31–48. Reference on p.42.
4. Raymond Williams, *The Country and the City* (Paladin, 1973), p.99.
5. English, 'History and the Refuge of Art', p.25.

Comparison might be made here with a popular writer such as John Le Carré, but in his books a meticulously researched world of structures and rules is created, a world which convinces above all by its unremitting ordinariness, and whose shape and conventions crucially determine the characters' fates. The focus in Keneally is different: for all the incidental detail in his books, there is little sense of an historically realised setting, more an *impression* derived from set scenes which suggests, without actually showing, riches of detail which would be accessible *if* the author chose to turn to them.

A noticeable effect of such reliance on detail is, as we have seen, that Keneally's central characters often remain as mysterious at the end of a book as they were at the start, even though we have been privy to various 'detailed' revelations about their diet, their manner of dress and suchlike private matters. Keneally's response (that human beings *are* basically mysterious, and that an author who seeks to explain away this mystery is misguided and doomed to failure) is only superficially convincing. It is in this area that the central tensions in *Three Cheers for the Paraclete* illuminate Keneally's later writing, and especially the unresolved conflict between that vision of a larger pattern to which the trainee priest Maitland seeks to aspire and the all-too-human flesh and blood individuals who constantly distract him. Keneally has referred to the debt 'beyond estimation' that authors owe historians for having pre-shaped the past, given it form and meaning. Such an approach to history (and to the role of historians) is deeply conservative, but reliance on another (and supposedly higher) authority for the grander structure seems exactly what Keneally needs to sanction his own concentration on the intimate (often shocking) detail; work done by historians of the American Civil War allows him to concentrate on exactly what happens when a man is shot, falls forward, and drowns as his own blood oozes into his hat. He is at his best directing the reader's attention towards the specific when it is clear that the overall pattern is either unknowable (in the hands of God – or Hitler) or has been charted by someone else:

> his attention engages most easily and completely with those epochs, occupations, modes of discourse, habits of mind, sorts of events which have an established, or an agreed upon, or a decreed structure. He prefers, it might seem, to deal with those experiences which occur within a frame or under main headings where they have been placed by processes of historical or philosophical discussion.[6]

6. Burns, p.42.

In the case of Schindler, Keneally encounters Leopold Pfefferberg: witness, survivor *and* amateur historical archivist:

> From the back of the shop he fetched a wad of documents. Leaving his son in charge, he dragged me towards the bank on the corner and talked one of the cashiers into photo-copying the documents.
>
> When the photocopies were finished, he thrust them into my hands. The next morning, he came to the Beverly Wiltshire Hotel with the lawyer who owned the rights to Oskar's life. When I read the photocopied documents overnight, I knew this was an amazing story. (TP p.346)

There is no denying that Pfefferberg was right in his determination that Keneally should read the 'wad of documents' – and that Keneally was also right in his assessment that it *was* 'an amazing story'. The account he gives is itself of interest, though, because it encapsulates so many of the qualities that fascinate Keneally, not only for the story the documents tell, but for how he came upon them. The account is itself a parable (to use Keneally's own term) of the way his novels germinate and operate: the chance encounter; the thrusting of the wad of documents into the author's hands; the author's solitary overnight reading; the final revelation of significance – and *belief* in the revelation: 'I knew this was an amazing story'. Belief in a cause, whether right or wrong, is a constant factor in Keneally's central characters, and it is the belief of the individuals he selects that enables them to assume a significance beyond the personal and temporal; allows them to assume the mantle of historical significance. Significantly, Keneally speaks of Oskar Schindler's achievements in terms that draw explicit comparisons with Joan of Arc:

> The energies which had moved him during the war, when he was a factory owner, black market operator, party-goer and -giver *par excellence*, and saviour of those who were by the Reich's decree *Untermenschen*, sub-humans – those powerful energies seem to have abandoned him after the war. Like Joan of Arc in George Bernard Shaw's play, Oskar's voices left him high and dry, vulnerable and almost ordinary. (TP p.v)

It may be this same need for belief that renders most contemporary Australian life so apparently remote from Keneally's fictional interests. His genuine love for the beauty and immediacy of his Sydney and seashore lifestyle, for surfing and for Aussie Rules football, is no adopted pose but the necessary human base from which he makes his forays into 'history'. It is almost unthinkable that a book of his should deal with everyday Australian life: all his books set in Australia, whether in the past or the present, depend for their inner dynamic upon a tension between that (more or less) immediately realised setting and a source of power – and threat – located far back in either national or personal history. The only possible exceptions are his 1979 'experimental' novels *A Dutiful Daughter* and *Passenger* (hardly stories of everyday life), and even here the power of Joan of Arc haunts the central female character in the former, echoing the full exploration of that (thoroughly typical) subject four years earlier in *Blood Red, Sister Rose*. In his only other exploration of contemporary Australia, *A Family Madness* (1985), the past of Belorussia is an almost omnipresent shaper of those aspects of Sydney suburban life we witness; in *The Survivor* (1970) an icebound Antarctic legacy haunts the petty intrigues of provincial Australian academic life.[7] All other major texts trace the shadow of international history, and especially the conflicts of global warfare, which place Australian characters and events against a broader backdrop.

Keneally's devotion of his talents to this wider history can be understood in terms of the role it played in his own early education, a role he himself saw as 'alienating'. His progressive definition of his own position, both as an individual and as an Australian, has involved an ongoing dialogue with the shaping facts of 'history' as seen from his perspective, and even when those facts have included Australia within their scope it has been in the context of an overarching (and, in artistic terms, crucial) colonial relationship which embeds local characters and actions within the pattern of publicly recorded and known history. *The Playmaker*'s focus on a convict production of an English dramatist's play on the occasion of the King of England's birthday perfectly illustrates Keneally's fascination with this pattern.

Such reliance upon dominant power structures is paralleled elsewhere in his work. A more detailed study of sexual politics in the novels than space allows would show Keneally's fictional world to be largely gender determined: men have responsibility, women have children. The apparently obvious exception, Joan of Arc, is problematic since her most remarkable achievements are attained while she is guided by her 'voices'. When Keneally does attempt an essential, 'ordinary', definition of women (and the collective noun is all too appropriate) it is often that stereotypical one which he gives to Ralph in *The*

7. For an interesting recent discussion, see Andrew Gurr, 'Is He a Camera?', Kenealley's *A Family Madness* in *Australian Studies* (Stirling), Number 4, December 1990, pp.13–121.

Playmaker, as he watches a captured Aboriginal react in terror to his first sight of the convict women: 'At their core, Ralph wished he could tell the native, under the layers of convict cloth, lies that same bounty of the womb' (Ch.14). The reductive alternatives of woman as threat and woman as fertile all too often define the options allotted to the majority sex within Keneally's fiction. As the Australian critic Frances McInherny has expressed the problem:

> Keneally's universe is obsessive and all the characters are trapped within a post-lapsarian and constricted world. What differentiates the male from the female characters is an authorial willingness and ability to examine the former as individuals. The men are offered choices; the female characters are made to respond through their instincts and entrails and have no opportunity for conscious choice.[8]

If Keneally's imaginative engagement with aspects of European and American history is well proven, the reverse can hardly be claimed. The rather bemused interest that Britain (and more recently the United States) has shown in Australia is matched only by their general ignorance of that nation's history and culture, an ignorance they have often sought to rationalise -- unconsciously or with malice afore-thought -- by attributing a form of primitive innocence to Australia, and to Australians. Endowed with this innocence, Australians stand outside the processes of history as representative of a more elemental morality; a distinguished British expert on international travel, no less, recently described Australia as 'a rather self-contained country on the other side of the world' without any awareness that, looking from Australia (even, perhaps, from the Continent?), this might seem all too apt a description of Britain. Such attitudes have long informed much reporting of Australia and its culture, and (shrewdly exploited by Australian actor and director Paul Hogan) have been responsible for the international success of the 'Crocodile Dundee' films.

In the context of such a tradition Keneally's position is far from straightforward, but focus on mostly non-Australian material -- and especially his preference for the blockbuster topic -- has facilitated his marketing to 'overseas' critics; his few Australian-centred books, meanwhile, have been admired, rather condescendingly, as exotic (to overseas eyes) evocations of his 'roots'. But as Robert Hughes observed way back in 1961, in his Introduction to London's Whitechapel Art

---

8. Frances McInherny, 'Woman and Myth in Thomas Keneally's Fiction', *Meanjin* (Melbourne) 40/2 July 1981, pp.248–58. Reference on p.249.

Gallery exhibition of Australian paintings: 'To think of Australia as a *jardin exotique* is a fashionable way of missing the point. . . . It is the place where we live.'[9]

That Keneally's own attitude to Australia is both individual and complex is indicated by the extent to which his spiritual preoccupations consistently locate the significance of Australian settlement, and of subsequent society, firmly within a Western religious framework of Western concepts of innocence and guilt. These concepts operate for Keneally very differently from those which outside commentators so readily attribute to Australia, but all too often are crudely accommodated within the latter. Keneally himself writes, in typically 'epic' terms:

> We have a culture that doesn't fit the land, or hasn't come to terms with it. It's a hangover from the days of our foundation. The Age of Reason came to a country that was different from anything that could then be imagined. This lodged in our civilisation a sense of guilt that has to be exorcised before we feel that our culture has an intellectual validity.[10]

The mismatch of 'The Age of Reason' and conditions in settlement Australia is true enough (it was a mismatch which applied for most people in England as well, of course), but it is debatable whether all Australians (even of Keneally's own generation) feel the 'sense of guilt' he describes as 'lodged in the civilisation'. Such guilt is lodged in his own sensibility, and is to be explained in terms of personal rather than national experience. He describes his own 'personal exorcism' as being *Bring Larks and Heroes*, where he 'tried to look at universal moral issues in terms of our early history', an enterprise which still evokes echoes of that early sense of alienation. Such an enterprise is certainly demanding, and the novel it produced among his best, but 'a sense of guilt' pervades Keneally's writing still. The problem, though – and it is aesthetic rather than personal insofar as it concerns us as readers – is that Keneally's work completely lacks any convincing rendering of the everyday:

> The condition which constantly eludes Keneally is ordinariness both in terms of event and narrative stance, because to sustain a created

9. Robert Hughes, Introduction to the *Catalogue* for 'Recent Australian Painting', Whitechapel Art Gallery, London, 1961, p.13.
10. L.J. Clancy, 'Conscience and Corruption: Thomas Keneally's Three Novels', in Nancy Keesing (ed), *Australian Postwar Novelists: Selected Critical Essays* (Jacaranda Press, Milton, Queensland, 1975), pp.57–67. Reference on p.63.

sense of ordinary reality requires him to engage in illusionism, to erect an analogical edifice which suggests the real through the intangible. The unseen is a threat for a consciousness like Keneally's, so that he is able to engage directly only with his own language, or alternatively to produce convulsive surreal fantasy, another version of subjectivism.[11]

It may be that a writer's ability to accept 'ordinariness' depends upon accepting also the immediate context of writing itself, upon deeming one's surrounding daily life a fitting and adequate subject for fiction. Such life is, after all, the present from which any past must be viewed – and have meaning, if at all. For Keneally, though, the present he creates with such dedication and skill is always *someone else*'s present, into which he has to imagine himself and transport the reader. There is a thrill in seeming to have 'a ringside seat to history', but it is limited by the very factor from which it derives: lack of historical awareness. Keneally's technique for evoking the 'reek and savour' of history, rather than presenting an historically-imagined analysis which would allow the reader to *understand* (rather than 'witness') historical events, seeks always to allow the action to unfold in an innocent and unknowing present; as reader, we know no more than Joan of Arc (or General Jackson, or Governor Arthur Phillip), and even our knowledge of historical events (that Joan will be burnt at the stake, that the South will lose the Civil War) forms no part of the interest Keneally invites us to have in such characters. Quite the reverse, his focus and technique offer them for consideration as our own bizarre contemporaries, different to some extent in dress and custom, maybe (in speech rarely so), but only too plainly our own flesh and blood.

In historical recreations of this kind fictional skill 'brings alive' characters whose *historical* existence is seemingly established independently. Authorial power derives from the presumed relationship between the two versions, or 'lives', of the characters: the one in the ongoing process of history of which we, too, are a part; the other in the recreated fictional world of the text. In this relationship, the conventions of the novel give the reader an access impossible in historical analysis, while at the same time allowing historical records to underwrite fictional options.

To share Keneally's vision of history as offering 'parables for the present' is to set aside any sense of temporal sequence; an all-embracing fictional present presupposes that any understanding derived from

11. English, 'History and the Refuge of Art', p.24.

our experience, or from studying the experiences of others, is less important than the sensuous 'reality' of the author's strongly-realised and intimately detailed world. That we know nothing more than these historical characters is, of course, a pretence; the present that is their world is itself part of what we know – an aspect of our past. Keneally's claim to authenticity is based not on factual accuracy, which he dismisses as relatively unimportant, but on access to those nooks and crannies of personal history that no history book records: we really *are* the first persons since the event itself to 'witness' Oskar Schindler dining out with Nazi officials, or to 'see' his reaction when he is given a gold ring made from fillings donated by his Jewish workers. From a hilltop unclouded by history we not only 'watch' the decisive battle of the American Civil War begin, but also 'overhear' the hopes and doubts of those involved in planning it; we supposedly hear the 'surpassing crack' of Corporal Halloran's neck on the scaffold, and are privy to his last thought – 'Am I perhaps *God?*'. Yet it seems ever more likely that it is Keneally himself who asks this: in offering the reader a detailed microcosm of the past, which is yet devoid of precise historical location, he reserves for himself a position of complete control. How well he uses this position remains the subject of lively debate, in Australia at least, if not in the endlessly-admiring columns of the overseas press.

The uncertain role that Keneally's writing occupies between history and fiction is reflected in the fact-centred chapters and other material (maps, lists of terms, copious acknowledgements) which, in various combinations, introduce and close *Confederates*, *Schindler's Ark*, *The Playmaker* and other books. In each case there is an attempt not so much to frame the fiction proper against a contrasting Preface, 'Programme', Epilogue or 'Editor's Last Word' (this, in *Towards Asmara*, after an 'Editor's Interjection' and 'Darcy's Last Word') as to erect a varied panoply of confirming evidence. It would seem that entering – but more especially relinquishing – the fictional world he creates is hard for Keneally, and that such go-between sections ease the transition. His wish to reshape the very nature of the novel is undoubted, and he has expressed his admiration for the achievements of Tom Wolfe in defining and extending the genre of 'faction'. Keneally still frets, nevertheless, at the very *idea* of form, his fundamental longing for a structured vision of this mortal life always liable to be overwhelmed by the unpredictable lure of life itself. Such opposing tensions do not easily make for tidy fiction, and this study has deliberately adopted a questioning and critical position; one of the best compliments the reader can pay Keneally is to engage fully with the problematic issues his writing raises – not only intentionally, but inadvertently.

Some readers may be puzzled, or even irritated, that I have suggested – though I trust not insisted – that there is much to be gained from locating Keneally rather more firmly as an *Australian* writer than is usually done overseas. My case is that Keneally's own geographical and cultural position is unwaveringly Australian; that it is scholarly criticism by his fellow-Australians that have best advanced our understanding of his work (however much he may complain – like Patrick White before him – about their lack of appreciation for his talents); and that such talents as he does have – and they are considerable, if uneven – are best enjoyed and understood in the context of a wider appreciation of the range and diversity of Australian life. This study makes no pretence to biographical assessment, beyond the barest bones, but when such a work is available I suspect that a more 'Australian' reading of Keneally will be accepted as standard; until then he and his smile inhabit a strangely ambiguous world at once apparently totally accessible yet very private. Thomas Keneally readers all over the world still know very little about him: in one sense that is right and proper, since authors speak through their work. But to the extent that overseas critics' inability, or unwillingness, to consider his possible Australianness (other than vacuous references to his 'lusty' interest in 'his roots') betrays ignorance about Australia (or, worse, indifference) the reader should be wary of trusting their judgement. As for Keneally, he will no doubt prove well able to look after himself, at home and abroad.

Chronological Table

1935	Born Sydney; 'unemployed until the age of five'. After some time at Kempsey, Wauchope and Taree on the NSW north coast, completes schooling in Sydney with the Christian Brothers.
1952	Began study for the Catholic priesthood at St Patrick's College, Manly, NSW. (Manly is at the entrance to Sydney Harbour).
1960	Abandons study for the priesthood shortly before ordination.
1960–63	Works as schoolteacher and clerk.
1964	*The Place at Whitton* published.
1965	*The Fear* published. Receives Commonwealth Literary Fund grant, which allows him to work on his next book. Marries Judith Martin.
1966–67	Births of two daughters, Margaret and Jane.
1967	*Bring Larks and Heroes* wins Miles Franklin Award; first major success.
1968	Receives second Commonwealth Literary Fund Fellowship. Lectures in drama at University of New England, USA, 1968–9.
1968	*Three Cheers for the Paraclete* wins national Miles Franklin Award in Australia.
1970	*The Survivor* (published 1969) shares Cook Bicentenary Award.
1970–71	Lives in England (at The Grange, Wimbledon) writing his next book.
1972	*The Chant of Jimmie Blacksmith* wins The Royal Society

of Literature prize and is shortlisted for the Booker Prize (filmed by Fred Schepisi 1978).

1974   *Blood Red, Sister Rose* published.

1975   *Gossip from the Forest* published, and shortlisted for the Booker Prize; *Moses the Lawgiver* (a 'book of the film') published.

1975–77   Lives for extended periods in the USA, lecturing in New Milford, Connecticut, July 1975–December 1976.

1976   *Season in Purgatory* published.

1977   *A Victim of the Aurora* published.

1978   *Ned Kelly and the City of the Bees* (children's book) published.

1979   *A Dutiful Daughter, Confederates* (shortlisted for the Booker Prize) and *Passenger* published.

1980   *The Cut Rate Kingdom* published in revolutionary magazine format (as a book in 1984).

1982   *Schindler's Ark* wins Booker Prize and *Los Angeles Times* Prize for Fiction; Keneally commissioned by director Steven Spielberg and Universal Studios to write screenplay (the film is still in production at time of writing).

1983   Awarded the Order of Australia (AO) for services to literature. Non-fiction *Outback* published (photographs by Gary Hansen and Mark Lang).

1985   *A Family Madness* published; Writer in Residence, University of California at Irvine, USA.

1985–88   Member, Literature Board of Australia Council (the Federal Funding Body for the Arts).

1987   *The Playmaker* published. Contributes Chapter 1, 'Here Nature is Reversed', to *Australia: Beyond the Dreamtime* (non-fiction book of a BBC TV series of three programmes). Member, Australian Constitutional Committee. Travels to Eritrea to research his next book.

1987–90   Chairman, Australian Society of Authors.

1988   Visiting Professor, New York University.

1989   *Towards Asmara* published.

1989–91   *Playmaker*-based drama, *Our Country's Good*, by Timberlake Wertenbaker, performed in UK, Australia, Canada, New Zealand, Poland, UK.

1990   President, Australian Society of Authors.

1991   *Flying Hero Class* published.

Bibliography

This guide includes selected criticism on Keneally and some comment which seeks to locate him within the context of modern Australian writing. The reader who does pursue Australian books listed here will discover frustrating truths about international publishing policy; many are virtually unobtainable outside Australia, though I have concentrated on those more likely to be so. I have mostly not duplicated here material previously cited in footnotes to my text; even so, the list is short for an author of Keneally's international fame. This book is itself the first to examine his writings at any length; others will certainly follow.

The most readily available exploration of some issues I have discussed is the Hodder and Stoughton 1989 'Textplus' edition of *Schindler's Ark* (indicated as 'TP' in references within this book); this has an Introduction by Keneally and an excellent collection of Notes, critical comment and relevant contextual material assembled by Terry Downie. I have not attempted to duplicate the references to articles and books on Keneally's use of factual sources, and wider issue of 'faction' as a literary genre, which Downie gives; some are indicated in the footnotes to my chapters. The other scholarly work most rewarding to read on issues relating to our constructions of the past is David Lowenthal's *The Past is a Foreign Country* (Cambridge University Press, 1985); this book has the additional merit of containing an extensive, and omnivorous, Bibliography and Citation Index. Robert Hughes's *The Fatal Shore: A History of the Transportation of Convicts to Australia, 1787–1868* (Collins Harvill, 1987) is a well-documented and very readable introduction to an aspect of Australia's early history immensely important for Keneally. Laurie Hergenhan's *Unnatural Lives: Studies in Australian Fiction about the Convicts, from James Tucker to Patrick White* (University of Queensland Press, 1984) is the best study of how the convict legacy has manifested itself in Australian writing. Keneally's contribution to the three-author publication *Australia: Beyond the Dreamtime* (BBC Books, 1987) was the first chapter, 'Here Nature is Reversed', pp.11–72; as an account it is interesting from both the historical and the personal point of view.

Writers in East-West Encounter: New Cultural Bearings, edited by Guy Amirthanayagam (Macmillan, 1982) includes a chapter (originally a paper for a 1977 symposium in Honolulu) by Keneally, 'My Fiction and the Aboriginal', pp.32–45. Other interviews with, and articles by, Keneally include: 'An Interview with Thomas Keneally', John B. Beston, *World Literature Written in English*, XII/1, 1973, pp.48–56; 'Doing Research for Historical Novels', *The Australian Author*, 7/1, 1975, pp.27–9; 'The World's Worse End?', *Caliban: Annales de l'Universitaire de Toulouse-Le Mirail*, 14, N.S., XIII, 1975, pp.81–9, and 'Thomas Keneally: an interview' by Michael Fabre, in the same issue, pp.101–8; 'A Family Madness' by Thomas Keneally in *The View from Tinsel Town: Sydney cross-currents in Australian writing* (ed. Tom Thompson, *Southerly*/Penguin 1985), pp.53–61; 'Thomas Keneally interviewed by Rudi Krausmann', *Aspect*, 4/1, 1979, pp.48–58; 'Interview with Thomas Keneally', *Australian Literary Studies*, 12/4, October 1986, pp.453–7.

Three stimulating general books on Australian history and culture, all available in paperback, are Richard White's *Inventing Australia: Images and Identity 1688–1980* (Allen & Unwin, 1981); Graeme Turner's *National Fictions: Literature, film and the construction of Australian narrative* (Allen & Unwin, 1986); and Christopher Koch's perceptive collection *Crossing the Gap: A Novelist's Essays* (The Hogarth Press, 1987). Seminar papers by international scholars on many aspects of Australian affairs, including literature, are published regularly by The Sir Robert Menzies Centre for Australian Studies, Institute of Commonwealth Studies, London; a wide-ranging paperback selection (edited by Liz Gunner) published by the Institute of Commonwealth Studies appeared in 1990 as *Aspects of Commonwealth Literature, Volume 1*, while a topic relevant to Keneally's interest in war was traced in *ANZAC: Meaning, Memory and Myth* (edited by Alan Seymour and Richard Nile) published by the Centre with the Institute in 1991. A useful paperback collection of essays on diverse issues in Australian history and culture, edited by the current

Director of the Centre, James Walter, is available in *Australian Studies: A Survey* (Oxford University Press, 1989).

A complete *Checklist* of publications by and about Keneally was published in the journal *Australian Literary Studies* (Brisbane) 9/1 May 1979, pp.98–117; this journal annually lists Australian work in all fields published worldwide. The best recent general works on Australian literature are *The Penguin New Literary History of Australia* (General Editor Laurie Hergenhan; Penguin, Australia, 1988) and *The Oxford Companion to Australian Literature* (Edited William H. Wilde, Joy Hooton and Barry Andrews; Oxford University Press, Melbourne, 1985). The other recent general introduction, *The Oxford History of Australian Literature* (Edited Leonie Kramer, Oxford University Press, Melbourne, 1981), is a stimulating but controversial interpretation of the terrain. Other general articles, or extended passages of commentary are to be found in W.S. Ramson (ed.) *The Australian Experience: Critical essays on Australian novels* (Australian National University, 1974, pp.329–44); R.G. Geering *Recent Fiction* (Oxford University Press, 1974); Nancy Keesing (ed.) *Australian Postwar Novelists: Selected Critical Essays* (Jacaranda, Milton, 1975, pp.57–82); Geoffrey Dutton (ed.) *The Literature of Australia* (Penguin, 1976); Geoffrey Dutton *Snow on the Saltbush: The Australian Literary Experience* (Penguin, Australia, 1985); Ken Goodwin *A History of Australian Literature* (Macmillan, 1986, pp.235–9). Other rewarding books are Brian Kiernan's *Images of Society and Nature: Seven essays on Australian novels* (Oxford University Press, Melbourne, 1971), which includes a chapter on *Bring Larks and Heroes*, pp.148–58; Chris Wallace-Crabbe's *Melbourne or the Bush: Essays on Australian Literature and Society* (Angus & Robertson, 1974). Robin Gerster's *Big-Noting: The Heroic Theme in Australian War Writing* (Melbourne University Press, 1987) is a perceptive exploration of this rich vein. For a personal, hilarious but also sensitive account of growing up in Sydney after the war it is impossible to better Clive James's *Unreliable Memoirs* (Picador, 1981).

The best single article on Keneally, which deserves an added mention here, is David English's 'History and the Refuge of Art: Thomas Keneally's Sense of the Past' in *Meridian* (Melbourne) 6/1 May 1987, pp.23–9; also printed in Kirpal Singh (ed.) *The Writer's Sense of the Past: Essays on Southeast Asian and Australasian Literature* (Singapore University Press, 1987, pp.160–9). Some general cultural and political implications of teaching Australian (or any 'Commonwealth') literature in Britain today are explored in my article

'Teaching by Example: Australian Studies and a British Education' included in my edited collection *Diversity Itself: Essays in Australian Arts and Culture* (University of Exeter, 1986, pp.5–19).

Literature by and about Australian Aboriginal (or, as some increasingly prefer, Koori) peoples is, at last, a growing – if small – aspect of the country's scholarly output. For introductions in paperback see, for example, Sally Morgan's autobiographical account *My Place* (Virago, 1987) and the critical study, which includes a good Select Bibliography, *Writing from the Fringe: A Study of Modern Aboriginal Literature* by Mudrooroo Narogin (the tribal name now used by Colin Johnson) (Hyland House, Melbourne, 1990). *Aboriginal Culture Today* (ed. Anna Rutherford, Dangaroo Press, Aarhus University, Denmark, 1988) is a lively creative and critical collection, which includes a 'Partially Annotated Bibliography of Australian Aboriginal Writers 1924–1987', pp.275–304. J.J. Healy's *Literature and the Aborigine in Australia* (University of Queensland Press, 1978; 2nd edition 1989) is an invaluable early survey.

Index